3.00

CONTENTS

STEAM ON THE KETTLE VALLEY

A Railway Heritage Remembered

Robert D. Turner

A PROJECT OF THE
KETTLE VALLEY RAILWAY HERITAGE SOCIETY
IN CO-OPERATION WITH THE
ROYAL BRITISH COLUMBIA MUSEUM

PUBLISHED BY
Sono Nis Press
VICTORIA, BRITISH COLUMBIA

Acknowledgements

Many people shared memories, photographs or other information to make this book possible. My sincere thanks to: Ted Alexis, Anthea and Jim Bryan, Frank Clapp, the late Eric A. Grubb, Pat Hind, David Holm, Jim Hope, John Illman, Bill and Joyce Knowles, Robert Loat, Dr. Herb McGregor, Bob and Nancy McKinless, Ken Merilees, Warren E. Miller, Betty Morant, Nicholas Morant—Canadian Pacific's renowned special photographer, Andre Morin, Glen Morley, Robert W. Parkinson, the late Eric Sismey, Joe Smuin, the late Gerry Wellburn, Wilbur C. Whittaker, Brian Wilson, Ted Wright and Floyd Yates. Thanks go to the Mike Osborne, Pat Hosford, Bill Turner and George Williamson and the steam crew at the B.C. Forest Museum.

Many Canadian Pacific and Kettle Valley railroaders and their family members have contributed to this book over the years and have been very generous, permitting me to interview them. Special thanks to: Frances Alexis; Athena Apostoli; Jim Barnes, conductor; Tom Barnes, dining car cook; Dick Broccolo, engineer; Toby Broccolo, engineer; John Favrin, roadmaster; Audrey Fulkerson; the late Gordon Fulkerson, engineer; Ernie Hawkes, engineer; the late Reid Johnston, station agent at Nicola, Beaverdell, Coalmont and West Summerland; A. Fred Joplin, division engineer and later CP Rail vice-president; W. Gibson Kennedy, agent, Telecommunications Department; Burt Lye, engineer; U. B. McCallum, conductor; Ruth Hansen McGregor; the late F. Perley McPherson, conductor and chairman of the Order of Railway Conductors on the Kettle Valley; Albert Martino, section man and shovel operator; L. S. Morrison, operator at Penticton and other B.C. locations; Ernie Ottewell, engineer; Walter Paffard, assistant superintendent; Alan Palm, trainman and yardmaster; the late Harry Percival, engineer; the late Til Percival; Jack Petley, Penticton assistant superintendent; Bill Presley, brakeman and later General Manager Prairie Region; Bill Quail, brakeman; the late C. B. Sharp, construction survey lineman; Art Stiffe, waterboy on the construction trains and wiper after the First World War; and the late John Williams, chief engineer, B.C. Lake & River Service. The Kettle Valley Railway opened 80 years ago; the experiences of these Kettle Valley people take us back beyond those 80 years to the construction days and cover all the years in between. I feel privileged to have known them and it is to these people and all the other Kettle Valley people that this book is respectfully dedicated.

Special thanks to: Dick Broccolo; Lance Camp; W. Gibson Kennedy; Randy

Canadian Cataloguing in Publication Data

Turner, Robert D., 1947-
Steam on the Kettle Valley

Includes bibliographical references and index.
ISBN 1-55039-063-5

1. Kettle Valley Railway—History. 2. Railroads—British Columbia—Okanagan-Similkameen—History. I. Title.
HE2810.K48T8 1995 385'.06'57115 C95-910534-4

First Printing, November 1995
Second Printing, October 1996
Third Printing, June 2000

The Kettle Valley Railway Heritage Society, in co-operation with the Royal British Columbia Museum, gratefully acknowledges financial assistance for this project from the BC Ministry of Small Business, Tourism and Culture. The publisher acknowledges the support of the Canada Council Block Grant Program.

A project of the KETTLE VALLEY RAILWAY HERITAGE SOCIETY in co-operation with the ROYAL BRITISH COLUMBIA MUSEUM

COVER PAINTING: Winter in the Coquihalla. A Kettle Valley train ascends the Coquihalla on a sparkling winter's day in the last years of steam operations.—MAX JACQUIARD

Published by
SONO NIS PRESS
P.O. Box 5550, Station B
Victoria, British Columbia V8R 6S4
Tel: (250) 598-7807 Email: sononis@islandnet.com
http://www.islandnet.com/sononis/

Designed by Morriss Printing Co., Victoria, BC
Printed and bound in Canada by Friesens

CANADIAN PACIFIC
PACIFIC

(Previous Page)

Gib Kennedy captured the essence of summer travel on the Kettle Valley in his beautiful photograph from 1950 of the eastbound *Kettle Valley Express* crossing the West Fork of Canyon Creek in Myra Canyon. An early morning sun catches the sides of the locomotive and cars. With eight merchandise, mail, baggage and express cars running ahead of the two passenger coaches, cafe-parlour car and two sleeping cars, business on the train had reached its postwar peak.
—W. GIBSON KENNEDY

The immense trestles of Myra Canyon, and those in Coquihalla Pass, were ever fascinating to travellers. After the abandonment of the railway, the trestles through Myra Canyon were repaired and made into an outstanding hiking and cycling trail following a tremendous community effort by Kelowna and other Okanagan civic groups, businesses and citizens. —ROBERT D. TURNER

Bill Presley, brakeman, right, and A. R. "Lex" Fulkerson, fireman, pose on the pilot of CPR Pacific No. 2649 at Brookmere in the 1930s. Bill would go on to several senior positions, becoming General Manager, Prairie Region, of the CPR before his retirement and Lex would become an engineer and a road foreman of engines for Canadian Pacific.

Passenger engines like the 2649 were not typical Kettle Valley steam power but ran into Brookmere from Spences Bridge when Coquihalla Pass was closed.
—BILL PRESLEY

Manuel, director of the Penticton Museum; Ray Matthews, for his assistance and photos from the Hutchinson-Matthews collection; Bill Presley; and Dave Wilkie. Christopher Seton helped a great deal with research in Canadian Pacific Archives. Many of the photos used in this book were very carefully printed by Chu Yeung or Lee Prouting. My family has always been patient and helpful.

Max Jacquiard, an exceptional steam railway artist, generously permitted the reproduction of two of his beautiful works on the Kettle Valley.

Institutions that have assisted with this project include: British Columbia Archives & Records Service, Victoria; British Columbia Forest Museum, Duncan; British Columbia Legislative Library, Victoria; British Columbia Orchard Industry Museum, Kelowna; Canadian Museum of Rail Travel, Cranbrook; Canadian Pacific Archives, Montreal; Glenbow Archives, Calgary; Heritage Photo Co-op, Penticton; Hope Museum; Kelowna Centennial Museum; National Archives of Canada, Ottawa; Nicola Valley Museum-Archives, Merritt; Penticton Museum and Archives; SS Sicamous Society, Penticton; Summerland Museum and Heritage Society; the City of Vancouver Archives; the Vancouver Public Library; and the Vernon Museum and Archives.

Peter Corley-Smith, Pat Hind, Martin Lynch, Randy Manuel, Nancy Turner and Dave Wilkie all read the manuscript and I greatly appreciate their advice. Peter also provided wit and insight during field work and many of the interviews.

Special thanks to Hon. Bill Barlee and the Ministry of Small Business, Tourism and Culture, especially Jim Wardrop of the Royal British Columbia Museum, for their support for this project. My thanks as well to the Board of the Kettle Valley Railway Heritage Society and Executive Director Joe Cardoso.

This book is based on numerous sources including interviews I have done with KVR and CPR employees over the last 20 years. Unless noted, all quotations are taken from these interviews. To make the transition from speech to prose, I have applied only gentle editing. My major sources were official correspondence, particularly of J. J. Warren and CPR Presidents Shaughnessy and Beatty, detailed reports on construction and maintenance, and publications from the CPR. Newspapers, trade journals and published sources were consulted. I also want to acknowledge the important work of Barrie Sanford in documenting the KVR.

The interviews were conducted in an informal manner, and I am constantly astonished and delighted by the clarity of recall, both of facts and atmosphere, by the people involved. While they were unaware that they were taking part in history, their experiences were clearly important and insightful and we are the beneficiaries. Their sharing of experiences has been generous and gracious.

5101

Introduction

From Penticton to Chute Lake in the Okanagan Highlands to the east, Kettle Valley crews fought a steady 2.2 percent grade. In the twilight days of steam on the Kettle Valley two 2-8-2s, the 5101 and 5251, were assigned to this *Kettle Valley Express* as it began the 27-mile (43.5-km) climb on July 9, 1952. The sound of their whistles and blasting exhausts would echo for miles across the valley. —RAY MATTHEWS

The Kettle Valley Railway extended across southwestern British Columbia like a large, often distorted, letter Y laid on its side across the mountains. The single end of the Y was at Midway, halfway along the southern boundary of the province. Of the two arms, the top one was at Spences Bridge in the canyon of the Thompson River, where the railway joined the main line of the Canadian Pacific. The other was to the south, across the Fraser River from Hope* at another junction with the Canadian Pacific, at a place first called Petain but renamed Odlum in 1940. The railway followed this route over a twisting, turning, climbing right-of-way that hardly ever seemed to run in a straight line.

The ideal railroad avoids grades, sharp curves, heavy snow and cold weather: features that can be tolerated or eventually evaded only at great cost. Moreover, it operates through, or to, areas rich in traffic. In all these aspects the Kettle Valley Railway, like the main line of the Canadian Pacific that preceded it by three decades, was different. The Kettle Valley blended all the negative elements on its mountain crossings, and over many miles of its route there was little traffic. However, in some areas, particularly in the early years, it became a means of helping to develop the population base, agriculture and industrial activity that in the long run was to provide much of its traffic.

The Kettle Valley Railway defied the topography of British Columbia. The elevation changes were almost continuous.† An eastbound train leaving the junction with the Canadian Pacific's main line near Hope began its journey at just 174 feet (53 m) above sea level. It then climbed to over 3,660 feet (1116 m) at Coquihalla Summit, just 36.4 miles (58.6 km) away, averaging 100 feet (30 m) per mile or, for most of the route, a steady 2.2 percent. The long, twisting descent to Princeton, interrupted by a further brief ascent over Otter Summit, dropped the tracks to 2,111 feet (643 m). To the east, over the snake-like loops between Belfort and Jura and on to the summit near Osprey Lake, a further 1,500 feet (457 m) had to be climbed before, once again, the train descended. From Kirton in the upper Trout Creek Canyon, the grade was a steady 2.2 percent down to Okanagan Lake. The Penticton station, on the wharf on Okanagan Lake at an elevation of 1,132 feet (345 m), was just 40 miles (64 km) away but nearly 2,500 feet (760 m) below the top of the grade.

Leaving Penticton for the east, a train would labour up 27 miles (43 km) of 2.2 percent grade to over 4,100 feet (1 250 m) at Hydraulic Summit, nearly 3,000 feet

* The town of Hope is on the east bank of the Fraser River but the CPR's original station named Hope was on the west bank. This station was renamed Haig in 1916 when a new Hope station was built on the Kettle Valley Railway in the town across the river.

† Elevations and mileages are from *Altitudes in the Dominion of Canada*, 1915, by James White. Mileages on the Kettle Valley and the later Canadian Pacific subdivisions varied slightly over the years, points of measurement changed, and trackage was revised. Timetables and other sources do not always agree. Roger Burrows' fine book *Railway Mileposts: British Columbia. Volume 2, The Southern Routes from Crowsnest to the Coquihalla* is an excellent standard reference.

(915 m) above the level of Okanagan Lake, before winding down through the West Kettle River Valley and at Rock Creek into the Kettle Valley itself and finally to Midway at an elevation of 1,914 feet (583.4 m). Between Hope and Midway, not counting minor ups and downs, an eastbound train climbed some 8,000 feet (2 440 m) and descended over 6,200 feet (1 890 m) while travelling about 320 ever-twisting miles (515 km).

Endless hours of hard, dedicated work were needed to keep the trains running safely through the scorching summer sun and endless winter snowstorms, and over seemingly endless grades, that could challenge even the toughest railroaders.

This book focuses on the story of Kettle Valley Railway and its steam operations from the perspective of people who worked on or travelled on the railway. It also highlights the long association between the KVR and Penticton and some of the other communities along the line. Each of the first three parts of this book includes an introduction followed by a series of albums and vignettes from the Kettle Valley story. The fourth part provides a glimpse of the future: the Kettle Valley Railway's heritage sites and the Kettle Valley Steam Railway.

Gib Kennedy grew up along the Canadian Pacific in southern British Columbia. Visits to Carmi and Beaverdell as a child and the friendship of many veteran railwaymen helped kindle a life-long interest in the Kettle Valley and the CPR. The CPR shops at Trail provided a fascinating haunt as a boy. It was a wonderful place for a young man intrigued by machinery and locomotives. He worked for Canadian Pacific's Telecommunications Department at Trail and Nanaimo, and also summer relief at repeater offices at Princeton, Carmi and Penticton in 1950. He gained an intimate knowledge of the railway, its steam locomotives and rolling stock. He also became an accomplished photographer, model builder and respected historian. Some of his beautiful photos of steam on the Kettle Valley are presented as a special feature of this book.
—LANCE CAMP

Steam and the Kettle Valley

"Did you ever consider a steam engine in comparison with a diesel and why people prefer a steam engine . . . ? You had your hot and cold running water on a steam engine; electric light, and you had the firebox door with coal in there and the scoop shovel was your frying pan. The little shovels are shaped with the little troughs in the sides. You'd put three or four pieces of bacon here, three or four more there; get it nice and sizzling and then you push the bacon up and pop an egg in each of those little troughs. Beautiful bacon and eggs.

"Then if you wanted a cup of tea . . . you could get straight boiling steam out. So you put your tea bag in, you pour in this boiling hot steam water, and you'd have a nice cup of tea. Then you decide you want to warm up some kippered herring or something, so you'd put them up on top of the steam turret; beautiful kippered herring. In the meantime, your potatoes, that you'd put on before you'd stopped, up inside the cover around the pop valve. You'd go up and get your nice cooked potato and you'd have a beautiful meal. . . . When you'd get on the diesel, you couldn't even make a cup of tea." —***Dick Broccolo***, ENGINEER

"I can hear those whistles still at night. They were going up to McCulloch, dropping the train and probably the pusher would come back to Midway and help another train. . . ."
—***W. Gibson Kennedy***, REMEMBERING VISITS TO BEAVERDELL IN THE EARLY 1920S

"The sounds of the trains out there, you can hear the noise of your own train. It seems tremendously loud and carrying. The whistle would echo back around the hills; it was very nice to hear." —***Tom Barnes***, COOK ON THE KETTLE VALLEY'S CAFE-PARLOUR-OBSERVATION CARS

Kettle Valley People

Kettle Valley railroaders: Dick Broccolo, fireman; Joe Collett, engineer; and trainmen Art Ingstrom and Jim McGuire at Princeton.
—DICK BROCCOLO COLLECTION

Section crews, including these men photographed on July 10, 1943 at Erris between Princeton and Osprey Lake, were responsible for maintaining the tracks and right-of-way. Each section was about seven miles (11 km) long.
—PENTICTON MUSEUM, 37-3304

The Kettle Valley Railway employed a highly diverse, hard-working and capable group of people. In the early years, many came from other railroads, bringing experience and talents with them. Some, inevitably, were characters who left stories that have grown with the passing of the years; others were quiet, shy individuals who went about their work with little fanfare. Naturally, the Kettle Valley railroaders had families and they too are part of the story of the railway.

"I started my first trip on the Kettle Valley Railway at 9 o'clock in the evening on December 9, 1915. We were 24 hours making the trip from Merritt to Penticton. So on the way in, the Trainmaster said to me, 'Why don't you stay on the road here, McPherson? . . . promotion is going to be quicker than any railroad in the world that I know of, on the Kettle Valley Railway.' It was 20 below zero when we left Merritt. It was pretty cold in Penticton, but not nearly as cold as that; it wasn't zero yet. So after I had a good cleanup and supper, and a good sleep, I felt better. I thought I'd make another trip. And every time I came back, I liked it better. I hired on as a brakeman on the Kettle Valley on December 9, and in February, I was a conductor. It takes some men 20 years for their seniority to permit them." —***F. Perley McPherson***, CONDUCTOR

"I started in 1924. Right here in Penticton. I was wiping engines; gee, what a job. I had to wipe the wheels and rods and clean up the cab and clean all the motion on the engine. Mostly 3200s in those days and a few 500s that were on passenger." —***Burt Lye***, ENGINEER

"The worst calls were s.a.p. calls, 'Soon as Possible.' Oh boy, I tell you, you didn't even have time to pack a box. They'd call you and they'd say 'Quick, they're stuck, or somebody needed something. . . .' Well, by the time he'd dressed, you threw your onions, your cheese and bread in the bucket. Most of the time you didn't even have time to make tea or coffee and he'd have to run. . . ." —***Til Percival***, WIFE OF ENGINEER HARRY PERCIVAL

"My granddad had the post office at Carmi and he used to listen for the train to whistle at Lois, which in a straight line was maybe a mile and a half, two miles away, but by track it was about seven and one half miles. But granddad didn't always hear the train whistle, because there were the little single-note whistles on those 3200s and sometimes the wind would be blowing the wrong way. Then he'd hear the train whistle for Carmi, which was one mile or three minutes away at 20 miles an hour. He'd get into a real tizzy and hightail it up the hill behind the store with the mail sack. I think the train crew waited for him many a time." —***W. Gibson Kennedy***

"The first job my dad got was on the section [in 1922]. Well you can imagine a green Englishman working on the section. He didn't last very long. Then he decided he was going to coal engines. They used to coal engines there at Midway in those days, out of a boxcar. They'd spot a 3200 on the low line and you'd shovel the coal from the boxcar across into the tender of the engine. The dust was awful. After a year of that he started to spit blood and he had TB."
—***Ernie Hawkes***, ENGINEER

"I eventually got on a steady crew [as brakeman] and being junior, that meant riding the engine. When you got a tailend job, that was really something. Back from the stormy end. Eventually I got on a tailend job with one of the best conductors on the Tea Kettle Valley, Hughie Johnston. He was tough to work for at times, but a good railroad man. He was awake 24 hours of the day. He'd keep you out of trouble. Hughie was a great fellow.

"Old 'Ring Ass' MacKay, Murphy MacKay, he could be mean at times, but he was a real good engineer. He could take you down the Coquihalla on a freight train, just like a passenger. Real good hogger. You wouldn't think he'd be working his engine, but he just had it in the right spot, coming up grade. Working the engine as it should be worked. I've seen fellows tearing an engine apart." —***Bill Presley***, BRAKEMAN

"Harry liked corned beef sandwiches. I had to make two lunches. One for going down and one for coming back next day. Then I had to pack two meals besides, for supper when he got in there. Maybe a can of corn, a steak, or a stew. If I'd made a stew, I'd put it in a jar. That's the way we had to do it. A jar of fruit, or maybe some cake.

"They were tough jobs, very very tough. When I think back now of the hours, and no food and sometimes nowhere to sleep. Sleeping on an engine for 24 hours, on the steel deck. You know that's the way they lived. They fried off of their pan; their frying pan was the shovel. Tea in a can." —***Til Percival***

"It was just like one big family. My parents never worried about us when we were travelling on the train. Any time I could travel alone, and I was quite young."
—***Athena Apostoli***, RECALLING GROWING UP AT TULAMEEN

"In the early days, when dad was engineer on freight trains, we just rode in the caboose. My dad was on the east run and a boyfriend and I were going to go up to Chute Lake to go fishing and dad said, 'Come on, ride in the cab.' The section men would always be out waving at the engine going by. And I was there leaning out waving back.

"When we were just real little kids, we'd go to the Coquihalla to go camping. We had friends who were not too well off and they couldn't have afforded to pay to go. My dad took this other family in the caboose and we all got off at Coquihalla. Even 10 or 15 years later you would never have done a thing like that." —***Ruth Hansen McGregor***

"Joe Ramond; Italian guy. When I was firing for him, he'd kick the guys [the hoboes] off the back of the tender, but he'd give them the money to go and pay the fares to the conductor. That's true. But he was a hard guy to fire for.

"I'd prefer to run freight; I liked the variety more. I hated yard engines. You were just chugging along, you're not railroading, you're just switching. It's a retirement job. I liked the fast road trips. I always enjoyed the Coquihalla—it was always interesting.

"Your first trip as an engineer makes you feel pretty proud. It was the pusher job up to Chute Lake. When you get the good word, it makes you feel pretty good. There's nothing like the feeling of getting to Brookmere, and you've kept an engine hot all the way over there. You're wandering over to the bunkhouse to go to bed and the conductor will holler something at you, what a nice job you'd done." —***Dick Broccolo***, ENGINEER

Ernie Hawkes started on the Kettle Valley as a teenager at Midway in 1934. —ERNIE HAWKES COLLECTION

Til Percival and her husband Harry, a Kettle Valley engineer, made Brookmere their home. —ROBERT D. TURNER

Engineer Bob Hansen retired in August 1953 with 38 years' service. He posed between wife, Emma, and daughter Ruth. Kettle Valley Division Superintendent A. J. Cowie is at right, grandson Harold Hansen is at left.
—RUTH HANSEN MCGREGOR COLLECTION

Gordon Fulkerson, after working on the Kettle Valley from 1916 to 1948 and the Vancouver Division for 14 years, would joke, "I never did like railroading." Audrey Fulkerson added, "He was a real smooth engineer." —ROBERT D. TURNER

"People along the way, in the outlying section houses and stations, were really hungry for fresh fruit and at our place we had these lovely peach trees. My dad, R. C. 'Bob' Hansen, used to take orders for peaches and mum would pack up a box, wrap them and crate them carefully, and then he'd be delivering them on his run.

"During the Depression years they weren't hiring anyone else. Through the union they worked out a system of sharing the work. He had enough seniority to have worked steadily but they were encouraged to lay off some runs." —***Ruth Hansen McGregor***

"I started in 1934 at Midway. . . . Right in the middle of the Depression and I'd hung around that railroad ever since I can remember. Howard Pannell, he was a permanent engine watchman, he had kids and he took a liking to me. I'd shovel cinders and he'd give me 50 cents. Boy that 50 cents in my pocket felt like a thousand dollars. He'd let me move the engine up to the ash pit. That was a real deal, I'd wait there all day for that move.

"Pannell got a notion that if he were to quit, then I'd get the job but of course men senior to me were just waiting for a position. You know, I think old Howard quit just for me but I didn't get the job. . . .

"Eventually they needed someone they could call in for a shift and I fell right into it. The age was 18 and everything was good and I was an engine watchman; $3.50 for the shift was big money. Eventually business picked up and the man who was holding the regular job went to Grand Forks and I had the job." —***Ernie Hawkes***, ENGINEER

"We used to have the 5230. You could play a tune on that whistle—one of the most beautiful whistles I ever heard on a steam engine. You could pick up that whistle anywhere. They used to come into Penticton, blowing at the crossings. They'd blow the whistles, the wives would listen to a certain tune, or something on the whistle, and they knew that their hubby was coming home." —***Toby Broccolo***, ENGINEER

"The engineers would prolong a note or make a bunch of short stocatto ones at the end. Some of the long ones would sound like a wolf calling in the mountains. People knew who was coming into town." —***Ruth Hansen McGregor***

"I went to school in Rhone, a one-room school there. Dad [Joseph Martino] was at Chute Lake first, then he went to Rhone. He was section foreman. From Rhone we went to Princeton and from Princeton to Oliver. I started on the CPR when I was 14 years old in February 1941 on the section. They couldn't get men. I went to Penticton to work on the steam shovels in '52. All over B.C., after the Coquihalla closed." —***Albert Martino***, MACHINERY OPERATOR

"You'd pull away from the station and the last thing you would see was the lights of the town, one or two lights, flickering on and off as trees would come in the way and then it would be just black. Absolutely black. No more lights. Just very few people at that time way up there between Hydraulic Lake and Chute Lake other than people who worked on the train. It was really remote. The people operating the little sidings, the people that maintained the track, they had a pretty lonely life." —***Tom Barnes***, DINING CAR COOK

The Coquihalla Canyon east of Hope presented some of the greatest challenges to the engineers and construction crews on the Kettle Valley. The four tunnels and two bridges are a spectacular example of early 20th-century railway engineering. One of the four tunnels had a large opening in one side giving the appearance of five tunnels, leading to the name Quintette. Andrew McCulloch, surveyors and construction workers were lowered over the face of the cliffs to work through the canyon. This site, photographed in 1919, is now easily accessible as part of the Coquihalla Canyon Provincial Recreation Area. —W. BAER, BCARS, F09818 AND F04508

Andrew McCulloch, left, and James J. Warren, right, were key figures in the Kettle Valley story. McCulloch, as chief engineer, was responsible for construction, while Warren, as president, managed the project and worked with CPR management. McCulloch, known as the "Chief," was born in 1864 in Lanark, Ontario and started with the CPR in 1897. He was appointed chief engineer for the Kettle Valley in 1910 and later was superintendent. He retired in 1933 and died at age 81 on December 13, 1945. McCulloch's many accomplishments are detailed in *McCulloch's Wonder* by Barrie Sanford. Warren was president of the Kettle River Valley Railway and, after the CPR's takeover and formation of the KVR, was president until 1920. In 1919 he became president of the Consolidated Mining & Smelting Company and held the post until his death in January 1939. —PENTICTON MUSEUM, 37-4613

Prelude to Construction

Southern British Columbia was first penetrated by the Canadian Pacific Railway in the early 1880s when the original transcontinental main line was built. Following the Fraser River the railway was cut through the walls of the great canyon and on through the arid depths of the Thompson River canyon before reaching Kamloops and the Shuswap. From the east labourers pushed through the Rockies over Kicking Horse Pass and then climbed the Selkirk Mountains through Rogers Pass. The construction gangs met in Eagle Pass of the Gold Range, part of the Monashee Mountains, completing the link with eastern Canada.

In the Kootenay, Okanagan and Similkameen districts just above the border with the United States lay some of the most promising areas in British Columbia for mineral development, agriculture and lumbering. By the mid-1890s, development south of the CPR was increasing. Steamboat services were operating on the major rivers and lakes and the Shuswap & Okanagan Railway had been built from the main line at Sicamous to the north end of Okanagan Lake at Okanagan Landing.

South of the border, the Great Northern Railway of James Jerome Hill had been completed to Seattle and branch lines and independent railways were being extended northwards to tap the resource-rich districts on both sides of the international boundary. Situated between two major railways, southern British Columbia became the focus for over 20 years of strenuous competition and railway expansion. By 1900, the Canadian Pacific had completed a new railway through the Crow's Nest Pass in the southern Rockies to Kootenay Lake and had laid trackage as far west as Midway, reaching most of the important mining towns in the Kootenays and Boundary districts. The Canadian Pacific's connections were not by a continuous railway but relied on both rail and steamer services. The Great Northern also had branch lines into most of these centres including Grand Forks and Phoenix and had the advantage of shorter routes to its main line.

In British Columbia there was an almost constant clamour for a direct Coast-to-Kootenay railway linking the main line of the Canadian Pacific with its trackage at Midway. The long years of dispute, promises and proposals go beyond the scope of this book but the efforts finally culminated in the construction of two railways. One was the Kettle Valley Railway controlled by the Canadian Pacific and the other was the Vancouver, Victoria & Eastern Railway & Navigation Company, the VV&E, a subsidiary of the Great Northern. Although the potential capacity of two major railways far exceeded the likely traffic of the districts, the early 1900s were a time of great optimism—and of railway politics. It was a period of tremendous population growth through immigration and extensive industrial and agricultural development. The years before the First World War marked the last great period of railroad building in the west as work proceeded on the Grand Trunk Pacific, the Canadian Northern and the Pacific Great Eastern. To the south the Milwaukee Road built its Pacific Extension making three northern transcontinentals spanning the border states.

Many surveys were made across southern British Columbia and the results all pointed to a route that was actually longer than the CPR main line. In addition, the projected line had several major mountain ranges to cross, which required steep grades. Consequently, without a strong economic climate and subsidies, the CPR was reluctant to expend a costly effort on construction of a line that would probably never be a bridge route across the province. Instead, the southern line's economic justification and viability had to rely on the traffic generated in the region through which it passed. Potential sources of traffic were important considerations in determining the route of the railway. Similarly, large blocks of lands, owned by the CPR as part of its land grants for building across the province, were situated between Midway and the Okanagan south of Kelowna. "The line," noted Andrew McCulloch who became Chief Engineer for the KVR, "was to touch Beaverdell and Carmi, was not to go north of Hydraulic Summit, and was to reach Penticton and Summerland." The final route passed through large sections of these lands but did not go north of them towards Kelowna.

Canadian Pacific acquired control of the Kettle River Valley Railway, a local line that built trackage from Grand Forks to Republic, Washington, and also up the North Fork of the Kettle River. The trackage in Washington, originally called the Republic & Grand Forks, operated under the name of the Spokane & British Columbia Railway. Along with this little railway, the CPR also acquired the services of James John Warren, a lawyer who, with the blessing of CPR President Sir Thomas Shaughnessy, was to oversee the organization and construction of the new railway to the coast. At the opposite end of what became the Kettle Valley Railway, the CPR had also constructed a branch from Spences Bridge to Merritt and Nicola, 47 miles (76 km) to the southeast. In 1915 it was turned over to the Kettle Valley Railway for operating purposes.

Another complication was the Midway & Vernon Railway, a speculative venture that had carried out some grading west of Midway and a token amount in the North Okanagan. This complex mixture of legal charters and underfinancing

Perley McPherson started on the Kettle Valley in 1915. Promoted to conductor in 1916, he worked on the railway until he retired in 1954. Perley died in 1979 and is still remembered all along the railway for his courtesy, warmth and good humour. —ROBERT D. TURNER

"McCulloch was a man amongst men. He had something up there that the average person doesn't have."
—***F. Perley McPherson***, CONDUCTOR AND CHAIRMAN, KETTLE VALLEY RAILWAY, ORDER OF RAILWAY CONDUCTORS

Troops have disembarked from the Kettle Valley train before travelling on the *Sicamous* to Okanagan Landing near the training camps at Vernon in this scene from the First World War. Amid the crowd and excitement, the train is backing away from the station.
—RUTH HANSEN MCGREGOR COLLECTION, FROM A DAMAGED ORIGINAL PHOTO

was eventually resolved by the CPR's taking over the assets of the Midway & Vernon. Federal and provincial subsidies approved in 1909 were another key to beginning construction of the Kettle Valley. The federal government offered $6,400 a mile ($3,977 a km) for up to 300 miles (483 km) while the province assisted with $5,000 a mile ($3,107 a km), for new trackage between Merritt and Penticton.

By 1910 the economy was prosperous, settlement across southern British Columbia was expanding, a subsidy was in place and the issues of charters and legal authority were all resolved. Canadian Pacific's operations west of Midway were consolidated under the name of the Kettle Valley Railway, with J. J. Warren as president. Joining Warren was Andrew McCulloch, an engineer whose name would become inseparable from the Kettle Valley story. Construction began in earnest that year.

The coming of the Kettle Valley Railway to the Okanagan and other parts of southern British Columbia was an exciting and welcome development for hundreds of people who saw in the railway the key to the future of their communities, faster and more reliable mail service and the possibilities for easier travel. These Kettle Valley residents, including Elsie Garie being held up for a better view, were watching the train at "Palm Beach," the swimming hole on the Kettle River near the station named Kettle Valley.
—PENTICTON MUSEUM, 37-0005

Trout Creek Canyon cut a deep trench into the benchland above Okanagan Lake. It was the worst obstacle for the KVR between Penticton and Princeton. McCulloch and his engineers spent days in the canyon to complete the surveys. Originally, it had 450 feet (137 m) of trestle approaches to the 250-foot (76-m) steel truss bridge. Later, fill and steel spans replaced the trestles. —PENTICTON MUSEUM, 37-2838

"Trout Creek canyon had imposed a big difficulty and it had been necessary to run a number of trial lines to find a good gradient."
—*The Penticton Herald*, APRIL 29, 1911

The deck of the bridge was 238 feet (72.5 m) above the creek. The wooden falsework supports were for the construction of the steel span across the canyon. —HERITAGE PHOTO CO-OP

PART I *Building the Kettle Valley Railway— A Construction Album*

Orders to Begin

"In May of 1910, the President of the Canadian Pacific decided to begin construction Midway to Merritt, and on the 1st of June, J. J. Warren, as President of the Kettle Valley Railway, and A. McCulloch as Chief Engineer . . . left Montreal for Grand Forks to begin work. At this time, Sir Thomas Shaughnessy in conversation with Mr. McCulloch stated that he wanted a good job done. He said further that this road would be a great help to the people of Southern British Columbia, would give them an outlet to the coast and, in time, might prove profitable for the company."

—***Andrew McCulloch***, *Railway Development in Southern British Columbia from 1890*

Many surveys had been made across southern British Columbia but much detailed work remained. The overall standards for maximum grades and construction were equivalent to those on the CPR's trackage east of Midway. Andrew McCulloch's talents as an engineer were quickly utilized in finalizing the route for the Kettle Valley and in determining the myriad details of design and construction. The KVR's chief engineer worked with other highly-experienced engineers in the months ahead including W. F. Tye and John G. Sullivan. Both had distinguished careers in railway engineering and held senior positions with the CPR. To J. J. Warren fell the task of organization, contracting, logistics and supplies, land acquisition and dealing with local interests and politicians. McCulloch's role was more dramatic but Warren's was no less important and the two men made a highly-complementary team. Penticton was to become the headquarters for the KVR and the base for many of its operating crews.

Track laying began southward from Merritt in 1910 and, the next year, work began west of Midway following the Kettle River towards the Okanagan. A third front for track construction began at Penticton in 1912. From there, with supplies brought down Okanagan Lake by steamer, work proceeded both east and west. By the end of 1912, 2,175 men were at work on four fronts. Grading was completed on 132 miles (212 km) of line. A materials yard had been established at South Penticton and track had been laid for seven miles (11 km) to Trout Creek. Overall, 85 miles (137 km) of track was in place and about 64 miles (103 km) was ballasted.

In 1912, the Provincial Government approved a further subsidy of $10,000 a mile for construction through the Cascade Mountains (sometimes called the Hope Mountains) and agreed to pay $200,000 towards the cost of a bridge over the Fraser River at Hope which was to carry both rail and road traffic. The agreement, for what became the Coquihalla line, also made the railway exempt from taxation until July 1, 1924, and gave it free right-of-way through Crown lands. Further Federal aid was granted in 1913 and included $250,000 for the Fraser River crossing. However, the subsidy was cut to support only 200 miles (322 km) which included the Coquihalla and Merritt to Penticton sections.

The line through the mountains to Hope was the final hurdle for the railway. The advantage of the new route between Brodie Junction and Petain was that it was just under 53 miles (85 km) long compared to 143 (230 km) between these two points via Spences Bridge and the main line. The disadvantages of the Coquihalla

Excursions and picnics to see the new railway were always popular. This group is at Chute Lake.

—PENTICTON MUSEUM, 37-2986

Pass became more and more apparent as the years went by. With the clarity of the passing years it was a stretch of railway that probably should not have been built.

This route, through the Cascade Mountains via the Coquihalla Pass, was formidable from an engineering and construction perspective and for operating and maintenance crews who came later. The major problem was the winter snows. In one year, 400 to 500 inches (10 to 12.7 m) of wet snow was not unusual; in 1945-46, 642 inches (16.3 m) was recorded. The snow and snowslides were bad enough but washouts could destroy bridges and bring entire hillsides slipping into the canyons. The twisting, climbing 2.2 percent grade on the western slope of the mountains coupled with the snow and ever present danger from slides presented a challenge to test the strongest will.

Complicating the KVR construction picture between Penticton and the Coast was the Great Northern's VV&E, whose trackage had reached Princeton, following the Similkameen River from Hedley and Keremeos, late in 1909. The Great Northern also had plans for a railroad through the mountains to Hope where connections were to be made with other GN subsidiaries in the Fraser Valley. This would have completed a railway connecting Vancouver with Spokane in the heart of Washington's Inland Empire. GN continued beyond Princeton reaching Coalmont in 1911, the trackage being opened to traffic the next May.

By 1912, both railways were positioned to build through the mountains to Hope and the CPR had yet to finalize its route from the highlands west of Penticton to Princeton and beyond. Expensive duplicate construction did not appeal to either the CPR or the GNR and by spring 1912 compromise proposals were being discussed. The Great Northern enterprise is another story, but an agreement, to last 999 years, was reached in 1913, and formally approved in 1914, that enabled the CPR to use Great Northern trackage between Princeton and Brookmere while the GN would use the CPR's route through the Coquihalla.

Meanwhile, on July 1, 1913, the Kettle Valley Railway was formally leased to the CPR for 999 years but it would retain its separate identity until 1931 when it became simply the Kettle Valley Division of the CPR. By the end of 1913, 254.6 miles (409.7 km) was under contract. Of this distance, 213 miles (343 km) had been graded and 163 miles (262 km) of track had been laid. Ballasting was completed on 104.5 miles (168 km). Work was proceeding on the Coquihalla route with over 1,000 men employed by McArthur Brothers, the major contractors for that segment, and the railway was advancing steadily to completion.

As crews worked to complete the railway in 1914, the world slipped into the catastrophe of the First World War. Its impact, at first slow, but with growing

Right-of-way Woes

"I never seem to be out of trouble. . . . Over in Summerland they are after my scalp because they think that I am not going to run through their orchards, and here you are on exactly opposing grounds. It is necessary for the line to pass through the orchards, but just where we have not yet determined. However, we shall buy all the property we need. . . . —***J. J. Warren***, IN *The Penticton Herald*, APRIL 29, 1911

30th July 1912

To: J. J. Warren, Esq.

Dear Sir,

I am in receipt of a communication from the General Secretary of the Lord's Day Alliance stating that you are permitting Sunday construction on the Kettle Valley Railway in the neighbourhood of Penticton.

I would be glad to hear from you as to the truthfulness of this rumour, as you can quite understand that if it is true you will have to see that the work is discontinued.

Your truly,

W. J. Bowser, Attorney-General

The Chief

"The Chief Engineer was BOSS. When I reported to the Chief at Penticton [in 1913] . . . I was startled when during this first conversation the Chief told his secretary to ask Mr. Warren to step in, for I did not know Mr. Warren was the president. Almost immediately a distinguished looking man came in and said, 'Yes Chief, did you send for me?' 'Yes,' the Chief answered, 'I want you to meet our new Resident Engineer.' This was, I think, intended by the Chief as a kindly tip-off." —***Henry W. Faus***, RESIDENT ENGINEER

Surveyors at work in the Coquihalla Canyon in 1914 as blasting and drilling progresses on the Othello Tunnels.
—W. GIBSON KENNEDY COLLECTION

"Dirt has begun to fly on the Kettle Valley Railway grade [near Hope]. As the first spade began work a mile and a half from town the dust was not noticeable."
—*The West Yale Review*, SEPTEMBER 6, 1913

speed and repercussions, was immense. Young men left the construction gangs and the railway to enlist, farming communities fell into disrepair. Immigration all but stopped and the apparently limitless growth of the early 1900s halted. Nonetheless, work on the Kettle Valley/VV&E joint line continued through 1914 and 1915. The opening of the railway did not wait on the Coquihalla construction. On May 31, 1915, regular service began between Midway and Merritt.

Each major section of the Kettle Valley presented particular problems for the construction engineers and work crews. The greatest barrier between Penticton and Princeton was the chasm cut by Trout Creek through the hills near Summerland. Although it required a major effort to cross, a lasting landmark was created by the construction of the steel bridge built to span the depths of the narrow canyon. Between Midway and Penticton, Myra Canyon demanded a myriad of bridges and trestles and presented a formidable challenge. Individually, most were not unusual problems, but the total collection of bridges was a daunting and costly undertaking which followed traditional engineering and construction techniques. Spectacular wooden trestles were needed to cross the two main forks of Canyon Creek. The tracks followed the sidehills of the mountains in a long curving route that brought the railway within sight of Kelowna but high above the town and the surrounding orchard and ranch lands.

Of the three major sections, the Coquihalla was the worst, costing about $136,000 a mile ($85,000 a kilometre). It required many substantial bridges and thousands of feet of tunnels. Ladner Creek needed a structure 600 feet (183 m) long and 239 feet (73 m) high while the bridges at Slide Creek and Bridal Veil Falls (Fallslake Creek) were each over 400 feet (122 m) long. There were many other impressive structures. Even minimal protection of the right-of-way during the winter and spring, required many snowsheds at anticipated slide and avalanche paths. In the Coquihalla canyon, the greatest single challenge was the narrow gorge of the Coquihalla River east of Hope near Othello. To carry the tracks through this gorge, McCulloch devised the famous Othello, or Quintette, Tunnels, which pierced the canyon with four tunnels and two bridges in a spectacular piece of construction work. Then, to the west of Hope was the Fraser River crossing, 960 feet (292 m) long, comprising four steel spans each 240 feet (73 m) in length.

The Fraser River bridge was completed in 1915. Gangs of men laboured from both ends of the route through the Cascades over the Coquihalla in 1914 and by the time snow ended construction in the pass late in 1915, the railway was nearly finished but final work could not be completed until the following July.

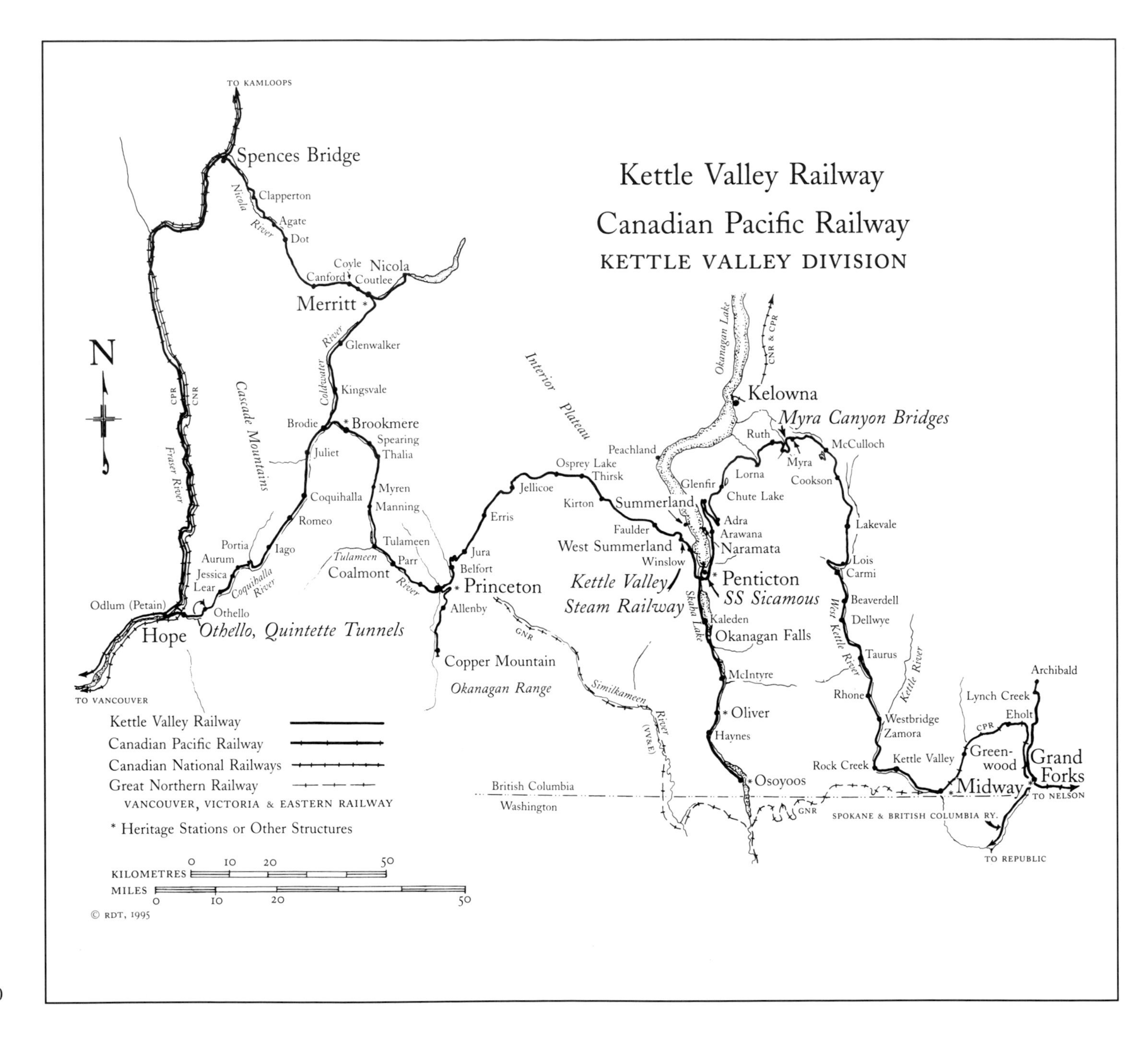
Kettle Valley Railway
Canadian Pacific Railway
KETTLE VALLEY DIVISION
TO KAMLOOPS
Spences Bridge
Clapperton
Agate
Dot
Nicola River
Coyle
Nicola
Canford
Coutlee
Merritt
Coldwater River
Glenwalker
Kingsvale
Brodie
Brookmere
Spearing
Thalia
Juliet
Cascade Mountains
Fraser River
CPR
CNR
N
Coquihalla
Romeo
Myren
Manning
Iago
Portia
Aurum
Jessica
Lear
Coquihalla River
Tulameen
Tulameen River
Parr
Coalmont
Odlum (Petain)
Othello
Hope
Othello, Quintette Tunnels
Princeton
Jura
Belfort
Allenby
Erris
Jellicoe
Osprey Lake
Thirsk
Kirton
Interior Plateau
Copper Mountain
Okanagan Range
GNR
Similkameen River
(VV&E)
Peachland
Summerland
Faulder
West Summerland
Winslow
Kettle Valley Steam Railway
Okanagan Lake
CNR & CPR
Kelowna
Myra Canyon Bridges
Ruth
McCulloch
Myra
Cookson
Lorna
Glenfir
Chute Lake
Adra
Arawana
Naramata
Penticton
SS Sicamous
Skaha Lake
Kaleden
Okanagan Falls
McIntyre
Oliver
Haynes
Osoyoos
Lakevale
Lois
Carmi
Beaverdell
Dellwye
West Kettle River
Taurus
Rhone
Kettle River
Westbridge
Zamora
Rock Creek
Kettle Valley
Greenwood
Lynch Creek
Eholt
CPR
Archibald
Grand Forks
Midway
TO NELSON
British Columbia
Washington
GNR
SPOKANE & BRITISH COLUMBIA RY.
TO REPUBLIC
TO VANCOUVER
Kettle Valley Railway
Canadian Pacific Railway
Canadian National Railways
Great Northern Railway
VANCOUVER, VICTORIA & EASTERN RAILWAY
* Heritage Stations or Other Structures
KILOMETRES 0 10 20 50
MILES 0 10 20 50
© RDT, 1995

Even when new, the Kettle Valley Railway was enjoyed by hikers and travellers for its breathtaking scenery and feeling of adventure. Dick Parkinson, at left, and a friend have climbed the Myra mile board high above the Okanagan Valley. The Kettle Valley's station names, particularly those reflecting McCulloch's love of Shakespeare, added character to the KVR that helped make it so memorable. Who could forget travelling through Romeo, Juliet or Iago? —PARKINSON COLLECTION, KELOWNA MUSEUM

Chief Engineer Andrew McCulloch recalled, "On September 14th and 15th, [1916] Lord Shaughnessy with several directors of the company and also some company officials including E. W. Beatty [later Sir Edward Beatty, president of the CPR] went over the road from Midway to Petain [the junction with the CPR west of Hope]. His Lordship expressed himself as being quite pleased with the road as to location and physical condition, which was very gratifying after all the trouble and worry in connection with building it. . . . The much talked-of Kettle Valley Railway was completed."

In those few years while the dream of the Coast-to-Kootenay Railway became reality, the world had changed. The impact of the First World War drained funds, labour and resources from many projects, changed traffic demands and plans for development. The joint operation by the Kettle Valley and the Great Northern over the Coquihalla route never materialized. Although for many years GN continued to own the Princeton to Brookmere trackage and paid its share of maintenance for the Coquihalla, it never operated revenue traffic over the route to the Coast. The two railways each paid the other 2.5 percent of the value of the shared lines which meant the Kettle Valley paid the GN about $60,000 a year and GN paid the Kettle Valley $144,000. Operations and maintenance were on a car-mileage basis with a minimum payment of 20 percent. For the GN this was a hefty payment with little return. Had the Great Northern developed a prosperous traffic base, the future of the railway might well have been very different. Construction of the Kettle Valley Railway was completed, and what often proved to be the even more challenging task of running this mountain railway began.

Unlike many other railways, the Kettle Valley added few branch lines to its system. Only three were built. The first, really part of the original Kettle River Valley Railway, ran from Grand Forks north along the Granby River, then known as the North Fork of the Kettle, for about 20 miles (32 km) to Archibald. The line was on a route surveyed to run northwards to Vernon and then to Merritt in the west. Because this subdivision and some Kettle Valley trackage at Grand Forks were isolated from other parts of the Kettle Valley, it was taken over by the CPR for operations after the First World War and was abandoned in 1935.

The second branch line was from Princeton to Copper Mountain. Built at the end of the First World War and opened after the Armistice, it proved to be a rich source of traffic although it suffered several lengthy shutdowns. Finally, there was the Osoyoos Subdivision built after the First World War southward from Penticton. Although it was not completed to Osoyoos until 1944, the subdivision became very important for the fruit growing and packing industry. More details of both the Copper Mountain and Osoyoos Subdivisions are provided later.

Railway construction techniques had progressed a long way since the building of the Canadian Pacific in the 1880s, but it still required tremendous labour. The first task fell to the engineers and surveyors to determine the best practical right-of-way. Then the line had to be cleared and graded, often with heavy blasting. Track laying and ballasting followed.

On the Surveys—"At the time I joined them [in the summer of 1912], the steel was already up from Midway to Beaverdell. Up beside Arlington Lakes was a construction camp and we had our meals [there] . . . and our sleeping quarters. They had camp cots, but in our engineering part, you had to break boughs or limbs or whatever you could find to make a bed to put your blankets on.

"I came into a seven-mile section with a resident engineer, and most of the work I did while on that job was working with a man named Louis, staking out the right-of-way. There was a prime line in existence and we had to stake out the right-of-way, 50 feet [15 m] on either side of that prime, centre line. In many instances we had to break chain* because of the steepness of the slope. But we got it and put stakes in every 50 feet measurement along the prime line.

"There were separate contracts issued; some to the drillers, some to the blasters and then contracts to the right-of-way clearers. One group of men was occupied in clearing the right-of-way of timber and growth; then along came the construction men, blasting the right-of-way, cutting down the hillsides and levelling off the right-of-way; and then there was the tracklayer and that involved quite a large amount of hand labour."
—*C. B. Sharp*, THEN A 17-YEAR-OLD LINEMAN

BUILDING THE RAILWAY

"I heard four-horse teams were wanted up at July Creek, $100.00 a month and all found. . . . I only had one horse . . . so bought one and hired a team at $30.00 a month. . . . The morning I loaded up, I was one of seven, four-horse teams, and made about two and a half miles an hour. . . .

"Then the snow came and we changed to sleighs. That meant bigger loads. The tote road from Kingsvale to July Creek was very bad, up and down short hills, chuck-holes, stones and stumps."
—*Ed Veale*, TEAMSTER

"We had walked through the uncompleted tunnel and were working . . . on the grade a few hundred feet further on. We had passed through the cut on the south end of the tunnel and noticed the men were packing powder in the holes for a blast . . . but away ahead of time we heard the explosions—a premature blast. The sight was terrible—several men were hurt badly and one or two killed."
—*Henry Eckel*, TRANSITMAN

In the summer of 1913 the engineering crew posed at the camp behind Naramata. Henry Eckel, transitman, is second on the left with Frank Hayward third. Resident Engineer W. H. Prowse is the fifth man. Later, Eckel worked on the Ladner Creek bridge and tunnel west of Coquihalla before returning home to New Jersey.
—HENRY ECKEL

* The country was so steep that the surveyors could not take continuous measurements.

Two tunnels were needed on the switchback climb from the Okanagan to the east. The longest, at 1604 feet (489 m), was drilled and blasted on a spiral high above Naramata. The explosions from the tunnelling and sidehill cutting could be heard rumbling through the valley for weeks. —KELOWNA MUSEUM

The tracklaying machinery, above right, fed ties and rail to the labourers as it slowly, one rail length at a time, worked its way along the grade. On a hot day, Art Stiffe, the waterboy, was the most popular young man on the railway. —VERNON MUSEUM AND ARCHIVES

With the Tracklayers—"That's me standing there, gazing at the photographer. . . . There is a gang on the end, keeps putting ties on the conveyor. Another gang are putting rails on this conveyor belt back behind. This boom is bringing the rail up here, forward. . . . They bring the rail out, the guys get on each end and lower it on the ties. Of course, prior to that time, the gang ahead has it all lined up; there are about 13 men there. They laid the ties down not too tight . . . a guy comes along with a wooden gauge to space the ties. As soon as the rails are put down, two or three guys, they drive the odd spike but they don't drive many spikes at all; a couple of spikes here, a couple of spikes there. Just enough to hold it and that's all.

"Toot! toot!, and she pulls ahead a predetermined amount and the guy signals Whoa! Good. Then the next ties are going ahead and the next rail come out. Of course they had to lift the rail from this side to that side. The boom swings over. The steam engine is behind. Old Gillis, he is responsible for not running off the track of course—he was a good engineer.

"A crew behind would be spiking. After the spikers get going, the line gang would line it roughly, not permanently. It's done permanently after it is gravel ballasted; to make it just nice you know. Then they dress it. Dressing it was smoothing [the ballast] from the end of the rail to the end of the tie and out a foot and then down.

"So as soon as they give the signal, away we go. And boy, there is no stopping. But nobody rushes. These fellows all know what they are doing. . . ." —*Art Stiffe*

"One morning, in the dining car [of the construction crew], they said, 'first train's going through today. Chief engineer is on board, Angus—the old boy himself—and mayors from different towns. . . .' No. 4 was pulling it and Sid Cornock was the engineer. I knew Sid Cornock well. I used to ride with him." —*Art Stiffe*

Myra Canyon

Between Penticton and McCulloch the railway twisted around the sidehills of the Thompson Plateau to maintain its grade, minimize rockwork and reduce bridging. In the end, it was a compromise: the grade west of Chute Lake was a steady, unyielding 2.2 percent, tunnelling and extensive cuts were needed and the bridging reached spectacular proportions. Above left is the magnificent trestle at Canyon Creek (now Pooley Creek) while the photo above shows the unballasted track in the foreground and the cuttings along the sidehills of the far side of the canyon. —SPENCER COLLECTION, SUMMERLAND MUSEUM; PENTICTON MUSEUM, 37-4582

Kettle Valley No. 3 was used on the construction trains but was sold soon after the completion of the railway. —PENTICTON MUSEUM, 37-3875

"Eckel in Naramata Camp. Tent used as office. The Chief and I slept here. Got cold in the winter but we had a good hot wood stove," noted transitman Henry Eckel on this 1913 photo. —HENRY ECKEL

Ballasting trains worked down grade through the tunnels above Naramata. This series of photos show the ballast plow being pulled through the cars by the Lidgerwood next to the CPR locomotive. After ballasting, the tracks would be leveled and finished, ready for service.
—HENRY ECKEL

Ballasting—"The Lidgerwood was a car equipped with a big drum [a steam-driven winch]. When the train was empty, a cable was taken right down to the far end [of the ballast train of gondola cars]. The last car had a big plow on it. They would run up to the steam shovel, and all these gondola cars would be in line with a steel plate between each one of them.

"They would start out with the track that hadn't been ballasted; the brakeman would ride on this thing near the back. The engineer on the Lidgerwood would control the plow. Now, at a given signal, they would start pulling the plow. As they pulled the plow, the train moved very slowly . . . a slow walking pace. All this time, the plow was coming through the cars pushing the doors open on the sides and the gravel would pour out. Eventually, the whole trainload of gravel would pour out." —*Art Stiffe*

The Fraser River Bridge

The Fraser River at Hope was a major barrier to the Kettle Valley. During low water, caissons were built and sunk in place where the concrete piers were built as shown in this photo from April 1914. Men, known as the "sand hogs," worked down in the caissons to remove loose material and blast level foundations. Armstrong & Morrison of Vancouver were the contractors for the concrete piers and abutments and the Canadian Bridge Company had the contract for the four steel through-truss spans. The doubledeck bridge cost $560,000 and was 955 feet (291 m) long; the railway used the lower level while the highway used the upper deck. A track-laying train crossed the bridge on December 30, 1914 but the bridge was not ready for traffic for several months. Other major steel structures on the Coquihalla section of the KVR were at Ladner Creek and Slide Creek.

—W. GIBSON KENNEDY COLLECTION, LEFT; BELOW, GLENBOW ARCHIVES, NA4457-3

To A. McCulloch, Esq
CHIEF ENGINEER

"Sir Richard McBride has asked us to take the members of the local Parliament down to Hope when the bridge is ready. . . . Of course, you and I will go along with the legislators for fear they might fall off the train. . . ."

Your sincerely
James J. Warren, PRESIDENT
24TH FEBRUARY, 1915

[a note on the letter reads "All off"]

Celebrations at Penticton
When Kettle Valley No. 4 backed the first regular passenger train from Merritt into the Penticton waterfront station on May 31, 1915, nearly everybody in town turned out for the event. A banquet, sponsored by Penticton's municipal council and the Penticton Board of Trade followed at the Hotel Incola. —PENTICTON MUSEUM

The First Train from Merritt

"The first regular passenger trains on the Kettle Valley line have come and gone. The real commencement of traffic on this Coast-Kootenay steel highway, to which Southern British Columbia has looked forward with undiminished hope for the past seventeen years, is now a matter of history, and Penticton is at last what she aspired to be, a divisional point upon an important east and west railway line."
—*The Penticton Herald*, JUNE 3, 1915

Kettle Valley Railway Now Open to Traffic

"There were gathered at the site of the station yet to be built in Peach Valley [West Summerland], a goodly number of citizens to witness the incoming and departure of the first train, with its load of passengers from the Coast and Similkameen, many of whom were going to Penticton, the official headquarters of the KVR, where the opening of the line was to be celebrated that evening."
—*The Summerland Review*, JUNE 4, 1915

"The fare from Princeton to Penticton is $2.80, and from Princeton to Merritt the fare is $2.75."
—*The West Yale Review*, JUNE 4, 1915

Coquihalla Construction—Winter in the Coquihalla presented some of the worst conditions faced by the construction crews. The opening of the railway was delayed until the summer of 1916 because of heavy snows. It was only the beginning of the Kettle Valley's troubles with Coquihalla Pass.

"They used to send me up slide watching. 'You're small, you won't start a slide. As soon as you see something move, just holler SLIDE! at the top of your voice so we can hear you.'

"I got there above the tunnel mouth. . . . I was up there for three and a half, four hours. . . . I just saw the earth starting to move and I hollered SLIDE! and grabbed hold of a Jack Pine. Down she went past me . . . pouring down, and buried the tunnel clean to the top and 15-20 feet inside on the track. I thought sure somebody had gotten killed. . . . After, Old Mickey tapped me on the shoulder, 'Well lad, you were on top of that, nobody got hit. We could hear you.'

"I was sitting on the pilot at the front of the engine, the 3120, holding onto that big pin, sitting on some chain. It would rock up and down, swinging and jolting. . . . Chug-chug; the old pop valves were going, the engine roaring through the tunnel. I was hangin' on to beat hell, wishing I'd never got on the thing. 'Lord, if I get off of this, I'll never get on another one as long as I live.' Around the curve there was a guy . . . flagging us down. Rocks on the tracks. As soon as we stopped, I hopped off . . . [and] sneaked in the locomotive. Then Mr. Sprague, the engineer, says 'Where did you come from?' A very quiet man; very grave. 'I was riding on the cowcatcher, Mr. Sprague.' 'Repeat yourself.' 'I was riding on the cowcatcher.' 'Never ride on the cowcatcher! Hell, if we'd run into a big slide around that corner, you'd have been squashed to death. The boulders would have gone right up on top of you.' 'I didn't think of that Mr. Sprague.' 'Well, think. Sit down and get yourself warmed up. What were you hanging on to?' 'I was hanging onto the pin.' 'You might have got your testicles squashed off,' he said.

"November and the weather worsened. Snow came down and cold. Nobody wanted any water to drink and I was up the banks everyday practically. My dad was getting on in years. Towards the end of November, we got snowed in a couple of times up the line near Brodie Junction. Locomotives got snowed in and we had a heck of a time getting them out. They wanted to get this snowshed finished to keep the materials coming.

"My dad says, 'I can't stand it. It's too heavy for me.' He was never built for this ballasting work and tracklaying. We were camped, I think, at the side track at Iago, which was about five miles from Romeo. There was a relief train going out from there to Merritt. If we could walk out . . . the train could meet us there. 'So if you are going to go, the train is going to pull out tomorrow at 9:00 at Romeo.' We got up at half-past three or four; cold, the moon was shining a bit that night. The track had been cleared off. The snow was crisp and crackly. It seemed like an eternity. . . . Going and going. I thought I would never be able to walk another foot. . . . All of a sudden, we rounded this curve and away in the distance there was steam going up. It was about 8:15. 'Jesus, we're going to miss it. Come on Dad, you're going to have to put on a spurt.' It must have been a quarter mile. We finally got there and the conductor said, 'We're not leaving till 10:00. Have you had any breakfast?' 'No, we've been up since half-past three.' 'Well come on in the caboose.' God, my hands were numb and my dad was white as a sheet. Sat him down and got him a hot drink. 'We're taking the women and children out from the camp. We can't leave them any longer." —*Art Stiffe*

Coquihalla Construction

Snowsheds on the west side of the Coquihalla were a necessity and consumed millions of feet of timbers. This is shed No. 7 under construction on September 12, 1915. Additional information on the snowsheds is on pages 74-77.
—W. GIBSON KENNEDY COLLECTION

A construction train and piledriver at work in the Coquihalla. A few old CPR locomotives, one KV engine from Grand Forks and four bought by the Kettle Valley were used in building the railway.
—SPENCER COLLECTION, SUMMERLAND MUSEUM

Snow closed the pass late in 1915 before the railway was finished. On May 11, 1916, the rotary snowplow was hard at work clearing slides at tunnel No. 3. The plow came originally from the Rio Grande Southern in Colorado, passed to the Great Northern's Kaslo & Slocan in the West Kootenay and then was acquired by the CPR, which sent it to the Coquihalla.
—W. GIBSON KENNEDY COLLECTION

"I was at Romeo in 1915 when the snow drove us out of the Pass in November, then trapped the two work trains with Jim Meldrum and Ed Sprague, loco engineers, and they had to send out for a rotary plow to dig them out. That was when they got the narrow gauge rotary that had been fitted with standard gauge trucks and a standard hood in front. It was a Great Northern rotary that the GN had used on their piece of railway at Kaslo and Sandon." —*Perley McPherson*, WRITING TO FRIENDS IN 1977

The Hotel Incola, built in 1912, became a Penticton landmark. The $150,000 structure featured 62 guest rooms on the two upper floors, including 14 with private baths. On the main storey, the foyer had maple flooring for dances and was highlighted by broad staircases leading upstairs. The dining room could seat 120 and a ladies' parlour, sun parlour, writing room and billiard room were other features. The large verandah offered sweeping views of Okanagan Lake. The cottonwood-shaded grounds covered 3.8 acres (1.5 ha). By the early 1920s, the hotel had lost its CPR and Kettle Valley affiliations and it was demolished in 1981. —BCARS, F03025

"The route is now being widely advertised, and next year we expect to take care of a large and growing tourist traffic. What we want, of course, is to induce tourists to stop off here at the Incola Hotel and spend a day in the district."
—*The Penticton Herald*, AUGUST 31, 1916

THE KETTLE VALLEY, PENTICTON AND THE LAKE STEAMERS

As headquarters, divisional point and the largest community on the Kettle Valley Railway, Penticton had a lasting and important association with the railway. Management and office staff, roundhouse workers and most engine and train crews made their homes there and the KVR became one of the major sources of employment in the city. By 1919, when Penticton had a population of approximately 3,000, *Wrigley's B.C. Directory* showed that, of the 550 people listed, about one in nine were working for the Kettle Valley Railway. The impact on the community was substantial. The other major employers were fruit ranching and processing which were directly linked and dependent upon the CPR's transportation system. In addition, others worked at the Kettle Valley's Hotel Incola (often known as the Incola Hotel), opened in 1912, and on the CPR's B.C. Lake & River Service steamers, which had been operating on Okanagan Lake since 1893.

The growing agricultural and tourism industries in the south Okanagan also contributed substantial traffic to the railway and Penticton became the main commercial and transportation centre for the south Okanagan. After the Second World War, the population of Penticton and other centres in the Okanagan grew rapidly. The warm climate encouraged both tourism and retirement in the area. The relative importance of the railway as a major employer declined but it remained important to the fruit industry into the 1960s and the lumber mills into the 1980s. By the early 1970s nearly all of the fruit shipments were trucked.

The CPR hoped that tourism would develop in southern British Columbia and contribute substantial traffic to its expanded railway and steamship operations. The construction of the Kettle Valley and the addition, by 1914, of three fine new, four-deck sternwheelers for the major Lake & River Service routes in British Columbia placed the company in a good position to offer outstanding facilities for travellers. In addition, two first-class hotels, the Kootenay Lake Hotel at Balfour, east of Nelson, and the Hotel Incola at Penticton, were built to expand the services of Canadian Pacific's already extensive system. Promotional booklets encouraged travel to the "Lake Districts" of southern British Columbia.

The Incola, initially built and managed by the Kettle Valley Railway, was considered a part of the CPR system for promotional purposes from an early date. It was situated overlooking Penticton's famous sandy beach and a short walk from the steamer dock. The hotel opened for guests by mid-September 1912.

Steamer services on Okanagan Lake preceded the opening of the Kettle Valley Railway by two decades. The Canadian Pacific built the Shuswap & Okanagan south from Sicamous on its main line to Vernon and nearby Okanagan Landing in 1892 and the next year completed a sternwheeler, the *Aberdeen*, for service on

"At Penticton, situated on the lower end of Okanagan Lake, there are special opportunities for beach bathing, sailing, motor-boating, swimming, fishing, etc., and the hotel accommodations are in all respects modern, as well as picturesque and homelike. No more enjoyable spot can be found in Canada for all-around recreation, particularly during the summer months.

"The Hotel Incola, at Penticton, is operated by the Kettle Valley Railway, and is an excellent centre for short or long vacations." —*Resorts in the Canadian Rockies*, *ca* 1914-15, ROBERT W. PARKINSON COLLECTION

"Penticton makes an ideal resort for the summer visitor, possessing as it does the splendid Incola Hotel, belonging to the Kettle Valley Railway. . . . All kinds of aquatic sports are easily available—boating, sailing and bathing. Penticton possesses a long shelving beach of sand that makes bathing a delight to young and old, experienced swimmer and novice. During the summer months, it is more or less in a state of continuous regatta."
—*Over the Kettle Valley Route*, 1919

Okanagan Lake. This vessel established the CPR's position in the Okanagan and gave people throughout the valley access to the railway. The sternwheeler services were expanded by the construction of the much larger *Okanagan* in 1907 and the addition of a large fleet of tugs and barges beginning with the powerful steam tug *Castlegar* in 1911 and the *Naramata* in 1914. The service reached a zenith with the completion of the palatial *Sicamous* in 1914.

Eventually, transfer, or barge, slips were constructed at the major shipping points. These permitted freight cars to be unloaded from the barges and run onto short sections of track right to the packing houses.

By the mid-1930s, passenger steamer service on Okanagan Lake was phased out when the CPR gained running rights for passenger trains over the Canadian National into Kelowna. The elegant sternwheelers *Okanagan* and *Sicamous* were both retired. The CPR's tug and barge service on Okanagan Lake continued for many years providing connections north from Penticton to Kelowna. From there, fast freights ran through to the main line to move the fruit crop to eastern markets. The barge service ended on May 31, 1972.

The *Sicamous*, approaching Kelowna at right, was the pride of the CPR's British Columbia Lake & River Service in the Okanagan. Completed in 1914, it was the last of a long line of passenger sternwheelers built for the CPR in B.C. It featured spacious lounges, a large and elegant dining saloon and overnight staterooms. Based in Penticton where it was photographed meeting the train in August 1934, above, the *Sicamous* provided a daily return service to Okanagan Landing. Passenger trains on the Kettle Valley stopped at the lakefront station.

In 1951, after sitting idle since 1937, the *Sicamous* was moved to Penticton for preservation. A major restoration program began in 1988. Later joined by the tug *Naramata*, the *Sicamous* is one of the Okanagan's premier heritage attractions. For more information on the CPR's Okanagan Lake steamers and the tug and barge service, see *The Sicamous & The Naramata*, a companion volume to this book. —PENTICTON MUSEUM, 37-1354; 37-3875

The Kettle Valley's yards and roundhouse at South Penticton, shown about 1920, were the major facilities on the railway. The big coaling tower dominates the scene. Engine 5204, at right, is shown about 25 years later. The roundhouse was demolished in 1986.
—BILL PRESLEY COLLECTION; JIM HOPE

"Four out of twelve new locomotives . . . arrived here on Tuesday. . . . The addition of twelve more engines will bring the total number on the K.V.R. line up to twenty . . . seventeen will have headquarters here. Each locomotive means a crew of seven men including engineer, fireman, conductor, brakeman and wipers."
—*The Penticton Herald*, JULY 22, 1916

PART 2 *Steam on the Kettle Valley*

"I never found out what a real thrill was like until I went over the Kettle Valley."
—CLERK AT THE INCOLA, QUOTED IN ARCHIE BELL'S *British Columbia and Beyond*, 1918

Few photographs depict the steam era on the Kettle Valley as well as this one from about 1930. Under a plume of steamy exhaust, an eastbound freight behind a D9 Tenwheeler, eases over the West Fork of Canyon Creek. —EDWARD CRUMP, LANCE CAMP COLLECTION

Conductor "Payroll" Bill Percival and engineer Angus Gillis, both Kettle Valley veterans, examine fallen trees blocking the tracks. The "Payroll" nickname came from Bill allegedly submitting a claim for a 25-hour day. —BILL PRESLEY COLLECTION

During its first years of operations the Kettle Valley Railway was formed into an effective and functional railway but not without difficulty or change. High operating costs continued and with the end of the First World War, many changes came including a depression as the world adjusted to peacetime conditions. The demand for metals fell off, Copper Mountain closed temporarily and the smelters in the Boundary District ceased production causing a further decline in traffic. The unhealthy financial situation of the Kettle Valley and major cost overruns on the construction of the Copper Mountain branch prompted CPR President Edward Beatty to direct in 1920 that D'Alton C. Coleman, who was also CPR Vice-president of Western Lines, become KVR president. The revised board was to include Warren, Grant Hall and other "expert operating officials." This restructuring of the KVR brought it clearly under the control of senior CPR management and a step closer to full integration with the rest of the system. Warren, who had become president of Cominco at Trail in 1919, directed his energies there.

Irrigation and settlement schemes for returning soldiers hastened the growth in population south of Penticton, a region with great agricultural potential. Oliver, named for Premier "Honest" John Oliver, and Osoyoos, whose post office was then called Fairview, grew to be substantial communities as irrigation, agriculture and settlement expanded. Fortunately for the Kettle Valley within a few years, the Copper Mountain mine reopened and ore and concentrates provided important traffic. By the late 1920s, the southern Interior and the Kettle Valley Railway were prospering.

With the Great Depression of the 1930s, traffic on the Kettle Valley fell dramatically, although improvement programs for the railway including two major steel bridges in Myra Canyon begun in the late 1920s, were completed. A major change came on January 1, 1931, when the Kettle Valley Railway became the Kettle Valley Division of the CPR and its operations were progressively integrated into the rest of the CPR. Crew seniority was a complex issue but was resolved through agreements between the company and the various union, or brotherhood, organizations. "Engine crews had B.C. seniority," explained engineer Dick Broccolo, "where train crews just had Kettle Valley seniority."

Declining traffic during the Depression years, combined with more powerful locomotives, gave the crews fewer hours on the road. The men who were low on the spare board could go for many days without work. The Second World War ended the Depression and brought traffic back to the Kettle Valley. Ore and concentrates, fruit and farm products, lumber and limestone all became important to the war effort. The postwar years were a period of prosperity and traffic on the railway grew but so too did competition from airlines and a massive expansion of the provincial highway system.

From its beginnings, the Kettle Valley Railway itself owned little equipment, nearly all being provided by the Canadian Pacific. Four locomotives, acquired secondhand in the United States, were owned by the company for construction and these were soon sold. In its first years, the KVR leased locomotives from the CPR, but the arrangement was short term. The general pattern was for the CPR to assign various types of smaller steam power to the demanding runs over the KVR. Typical early engines were aging classes of 2-8-0s (CPR's 3100 and 3200 series) "demoted" from mainline service by newer, more powerful and efficient machines. The 3200 2-8-0s worked most assignments on the Kettle Valley through the 1920s until most were replaced by similar, although newer and heavier, 3400 and a few 3500 series locomotives. The 3400 2-8-0s were common on the Kettle Valley, with some being assigned there in the early and mid 1920s. During the 1920s, passenger trains and some lighter freight runs were also assigned to Tenwheelers from the CPR's D9 class.

As traffic increased and as more powerful locomotives were available, equipment on the Kettle Valley was improved. Usually new engines for the main line meant some better, but often still quite old, power for the KVR. However, heavier locomotives could not simply be sent to the KVR because often bridges had to be strengthened.

A major change in locomotives on the Kettle Valley came in the early 1930s with the introduction of more 2-8-0s in the 3600, and later, the 3700 classes. A 2-8-0 was not a typical North American passenger locomotive, but this type was used in this role routinely on the Kettle Valley and on the Kootenay Division to the east. Speed was not a primary concern and the pulling abilities of the Consolidations was more important. However, as trains grew in length, more powerful locomotives, with greater steaming capacity, were needed.

In 1932, the CPR assigned more modern locomotives to the Kettle Valley and Kootenay divisions in the form of the 5100, P1d and P1e, class 2-8-2s. In August, the 5120 and 5178 were assigned to the Vancouver-Penticton passenger trains and soon others followed, some working out of Nelson. Some of the first P1s were oil-burners, transferred from the main line. However most were coal-burners.

At Midway, a young woman and soldier pose with a KVR railwayman on the pilot of the 3214 about 1918. —BILL PRESLEY

From Princeton to Brookmere, the Kettle Valley followed the Tulameen River and Otter Creek on Great Northern trackage, towards the Cascade Mountains. The railway passed through the mining town of Coalmont and the community of Tulameen at the south end of Otter Lake. There, in the winter months, hundreds of carloads of ice were harvested for the Great Northern and moved by train to Wenatchee to cool the next season's fruit crop during shipment. This beautiful photo, from the late 1920s, captures the westbound passenger train, headed by a D9 Tenwheeler, near Coalmont. —BILL PRESLEY COLLECTION

The Kettle Valley's Penticton station which also housed the railway's main office, was next to the steamer wharf and was often the busiest place in the city. It was located across from the Hotel Incola and adjacent to the business district. Here No. 3405 is on the headend of the passenger train, which has been backed down to the station from South Penticton.
—VANCOUVER PUBLIC LIBRARY, 13653

Outside Penticton's second station, a crew switches freight cars in the South Penticton yards. The 3487, shown on April 7, 1943, was typical of Kettle Valley freight engines from the mid-1920s until the arrival of heavier locomotives in the early 1930s. Some 3400s continued on the Kettle Valley through the mid-1940s.
—JIM HOPE

After the end of daily passenger service on the *Sicamous* in 1935, there was little need for passenger trains to stop at the lakefront station. This new building was completed at the rail yards south of town in December 1941. Later expanded, at a cost of $50,000, it survived the demise of the railway to become a community centre in the 1990s. —LUMB STOCKS PHOTO, PENTICTON MUSEUM

Shorn of its pilot wheels for use in the yards, the 3448 and crew were kept busy handling the fruit shipments passing through Penticton on October 3, 1947. —JIM HOPE

Initially they were hand-fired but eventually mechanical stokers were fitted, which took away much of the burden on the firemen trying to keep steam up on the mountain grades. Later, all of these Kettle Valley engines were converted to burn oil. Surprisingly, after a year or two, at least four of the 3600s were assigned back to the passenger service between Nelson and Midway. First the 3606 and 3687, and soon after, the 3602 and 3683 were nicely decorated with a gold band around the sides of their tenders, white running boards and tires. Within a few years, the passenger service 2-8-0s returned to freight assignments, although 2-8-0s would still occasionally run on passenger trains.

Passenger trains grew considerably in length over the years of steam operations. While early trains were usually just four cars, by the late 1940s 10 cars was more common and sometimes, when there was a lot of express and other head-end business, trains could be as long as 15 cars. Naturally these long trains required more power and the P1 2-8-2s were ideal. In the late 1940s, P1n class, 5200, 2-8-2s came to the Kettle Valley. They were rebuilt from 3600 or 3700 2-8-0s. This program to modernize and extend the life of aging 2-8-0s began in 1946 and continued through 1949. However, because the Kettle Valley and Kootenay divisions were dieselized so early, the P1ns that were assigned to southern British Columbia, operated there for only a few years before being sent elsewhere to work out their last years.

Locomotive assignments were far from cast in stone. A Royal Hudson, the now famous 2860, apparently took its train as far as Brookmere during a time when the main line was blocked. However, its long wheelbase and weight made it unsuitable for any further operations. Some 4-6-2s in the CPR's 2500 and 2600 series also operated into Brookmere, particularly when traffic was diverted through Spences Bridge. Larger 2700s were also tried out on the Kettle Valley but the high-drivered Pacifics, at home on the main line, were really not well adapted to the sharp curves and 2.2 percent grades of the southern Interior, where slow speed was the norm. Heavier trains, which in any case required a helper, made the use of the Pacifics practical as far east as Penticton.

Once an engine was assigned to a particular area for operations, it often stayed there for many years and would become an old friend if the engine crews were lucky or antagonist if they were not, depending on its characteristics. For anyone at trackside an engine, with its crew and the train crew in the caboose, could become a familiar sight and an anticipated friendly passerby every day or so. Most engineers and firemen had their favourite locomotives and looked upon others with distaste and occasionally downright disgust. Some would run like fine watches. The 3256 was called "a racehorse" because its valves were perfectly set up. Others might be difficult to fire or could be very rough-riding. Some seemed to have a penchant for accidents and wrecks. The early locomotives, the 3100s and 3200s, had boilers that extended right to the back of the wooden cab. These "deckless" engines were uncomfortable to work, and engineers and fireman could be baked by the heat from the boiler on one side and frozen by the cold and wind on the other. They could also be dangerous in the event of a derailment because there was so little space in the cab that the engine crew could be crushed, or scalded by any ruptures in the steam pipes or appliances. The construction of deckless engines was discontinued in the early 1900s for safety reasons, but many older machines survived for decades.

Almost invariably, locomotives were known by their numbers. The hefty 2-8-0s were the "thirty-sixes" or the "thirty-six hundreds." Individual engines were the known as, for example, "the thirty-two fifty-six," or the "five seventy-one," never as the "three-two-five-six" or the "five hundred and seventy-one." Of course some engines acquired names that remain unprintable.

Sometimes locomotives would disappear for a time when they were needed elsewhere or were due for a major overhaul, but they usually came back for more seasons of work on the KVR. Some husky oldtimers, all dating from 1899 or 1900, worked Kettle Valley trains from 1916 or 1917 until the late 1920s. In contrast, other locomotives might appear for a month or two and then be assigned elsewhere. Over the years dozens of locomotives worked over the Kettle Valley. Some are well recorded and others left little or nothing to recall their passage.

Kettle Valley railroaders sometimes felt they received only the castoffs from the CPR but in fairness, Kettle Valley power, when replaced, usually found its way to other CPR operations. "It could have been a good railroad, but all the junk went to the Kettle Valley. Worst engines in the country," commented one engineer echoing the sentiments of some of his contemporaries. Kettle Valley crews may not have appreciated all their aging machines but they were not the last railroaders to work them, and despite the apparent disgust, it was more bluster than serious and engineers would still recall certain machines with great fondness.

The assignments and operations of locomotives varied with traffic demands and the evolving needs of customers. Penticton was the major terminal for engines and crews working trains east to Midway and west to Princeton, Brookmere and Hope. On the east side, Kettle Valley crews did not normally run beyond Midway. CPR crews brought trains west from Nelson or Grand Forks to Midway and took over eastbound trains from the Kettle Valley. Penticton crews

The Coquihalla River flooded in 1932. This photo shows the Kettle Valley's crossing with the Canadian National near Hope. The Kettle Valley tracks run from left to right in the photo. The interlocking signals, which controlled the movement of trains, were operated from the signal tower. —ENSTROM COLLECTION, HOPE MUSEUM

"You weren't very often bored, especially working down on the Coquihalla. You're on top of the trains on the 2 percent grades, you had to be pretty catty because you are going over the top of the train all the time on the move. You set up the retainers and you'd always take them down on the fly. You'd go along the top and knock them off. You got so you had pretty good balance." —*Jim Barnes*, BRAKEMAN

Section crews took great pride in their work. This piece of newly lifted track, with perfectly trimmed ballast, was the work of John Favrin and his section crew near Chute Lake, Mileage 110.7, in the late 1940s. —JOHN FAVRIN

Conductor's or tailend brakeman's view of a short freight crossing Canyon Creek in the 1920s. —SPENCER COLLECTION, SUMMERLAND MUSEUM

going west usually ran to Brookmere, booked rest, and then returned home. Other crews at Brookmere worked over the Coquihalla to Hope (and later to Ruby Creek) and back. From Hope or Ruby Creek west to Vancouver, CPR crews once again handled the tonnage. After the Kettle Valley became a division of the CPR in 1931, Brookmere crews ran through to Ruby Creek on the CPR main line and Hope was not used as a terminal although facilities, including a small engine house, were still maintained there.

Passenger train engines were operated somewhat differently from freight locomotives after the KV Division was formed. Nelson engines were run through to Penticton instead of turning over the *Kootenay Express* to Kettle Valley engines at Midway. At Penticton they were turned around to take the *Kettle Valley Express* eastbound. Penticton or Vancouver engines were assigned to the trains between Penticton and Vancouver. Engine crews, however, still changed at Midway, Penticton or Brookmere and train crews at Penticton.

Helpers and wayfreight engines were also based at Brookmere or Princeton. Pusher operations were an everyday facet of railroading on the Kettle Valley Division. They were required on passenger and freight assignments across the southern Interior. Passenger trains running eastbound from Vancouver took on a helper at Hope that ran to Brookmere and again at Princeton that assisted the train to Jura. At Penticton a helper was again needed for the climb to Chute Lake. Further east, helpers were needed again between Midway and Eholt, and yet again east of Grand Forks for the long pull over the mountains between Cascade and Farron before the descent to Castlegar.

Westbound, the story was similar although grades were not quite so demanding. Helpers were assigned to most passenger trains from Labarthe, west of Castlegar, to Farron, Grand Forks to Eholt and Penticton to Kirton. Freights usually had helpers both ways over the Coquihalla although these worked harder on the climb from the west. Westbound trains often had a helper simply to move the engine back to the other side of the mountains. Helpers were usually run on freights eastbound from Penticton as far as Chute Lake. Westbound freights did not normally need assistance but between Midway and McCulloch crews often worked an extra turn, or trip, to McCulloch and back to Midway before enough tonnage was built up at the summit to complete the run to Penticton.

Typical helper locomotives from the 1930s until the end of steam were tough and reliable N2 class 2-8-0s but Penticton also had some heavier machines assigned in the early 1940s. These were one or two of the R3d class 2-10-0s. Slow but powerful engines, they were placed on heavy trains to assist the road engines up the steep grades out of the Okanagan Valley. Most switching assignments on the Kettle Valley were performed by the wayfreight and freight crews using their road locomotives. The only yard regularly assigned engines was Penticton where an older road engine not powerful enough to handle the long trains of the post-Second World War period, performed the low-speed switching chores. The Kettle Valley saw few steam switchers although an 0-8-0, rebuilt from a 3500 2-8-0 in 1928, was assigned to the Penticton yard in later years.

For the first 35 years of operations, locomotives on the Kettle Valley with few exceptions, like most other CPR steam engines, burned coal. Major deposits in the Nicola Valley, at Coalmont, at Bankhead in Alberta, on Vancouver Island and in the Crowsnest Pass assured cheap, if often dirty, supplies of fuel. Kettle Valley crews usually worked with Nicola coal until the mines closed in the mid-1940s. Fireman disliked it for its ash and the difficulty it presented in keeping a good fire burning. "Bull Durham" was one printable name applied to it. Occasionally, coal from Vancouver Island would be available and it was considered superior.

Beginning in 1949 nearly all Kettle Valley Division steam locomotives were converted to burn oil following an agreement with a major oil company over stable pricing and a payment to the CPR of $3,500 towards the cost of each conversion. The change brought considerable savings, gave greater fuel efficiency and was certainly a boon to the engine crews. The hand-firing of coal-burners on heavy trains over the steep grades had long been the bane of the firemen's existence and the union had lobbied long and hard for improved conditions and the assignment of stoker-equipped engines or oil burners.

As the 1950s dawned, the Kettle Valley Division was busy with increasing traffic and substantial improvements were made to the railway. Passenger services included the daily *Kootenay Express*, Train No. 11, westbound and the eastbound No. 12, the *Kettle Valley Express*. These trains ran between Vancouver and Medicine Hat, on the CPR main line, in southeastern Alberta. In addition, Trains 45 and 46, instituted in 1947, operating on a complementary schedule, ran daily between Vancouver and Penticton. They were intended to move fresh fruit to the Pacific coast and at the same time expand passenger service in the busy post-Second World War years. As well, there was a mixed train running three days a week connecting Brookmere with Merritt and Spences Bridge.

Although the passenger service appeared healthy, with ten-car trains being common, the business reflected an increase in express freight, mail and perishables more than passenger travel. In 1946, Passenger Merchandise Service freight cars were included in the passenger trains to expedite delivery of small shipments

Kettle Valley veterans Charlie Craney, engineer, and George Thom, conductor, check their train orders.
—PENTICTON MUSEUM, 37-354

Paddy Ahlgren was operator at Brookmere and one of the few women who worked on the Kettle Valley.
—JIM BARNES COLLECTION

Never Excite a Lion

"We were picking up the circus train from CN at Hope. . . . We had to run back to get the cars with the animals. The engineer started winding her up pretty good. . . . I piled onto the flatcar, with one stirrup and one grab iron, hanging on and leaning out. As we pounded out over the frog, Boom! Boom! Boom!, there was a hell of a RRRooorrr! from this lion right above me: Shit from head to toe!

"They wouldn't let me on the engine or caboose. I rode the damned tender to Iago. . . . It was breaking dawn, and those lions started to roar in that close canyon; you wouldn't believe the echoes. I think every billygoat for 100 miles was scared to death!" —*Alan Palm*, BRAKEMAN

The Jitney . . .

"It was a fun job. The passengers were mostly Indians and cowboys from the different ranches. They'd hop on the Jitney at Merritt and go to the next station down the line or maybe to Spences Bridge. They'd go to get groceries and come back. You got to know people all along the Coldwater. There was lumber from little mills, loads of horses, and express and mail. You stopped at every station and got out of every train's way. No rush. The coach was pretty basic—a combination coach and baggage built about 1910." —*Jim Barnes*, BRAKEMAN

in hopes of competing more effectively with trucking. Normally three of four of these cars were included in Trains 11 and 12. Unfortunately, this type of business was particularly vulnerable to competition from trucking and the airlines and by the mid-1950s, Canadian Pacific itself was trucking much of this business.

Through freight trains between the main line junctions at either Ruby Creek or Spences Bridge and Nelson and points east were operated on a daily schedule in each direction. Wayfreights, which served industries along the lines, were normally dispatched three days a week in each direction over the Princeton Subdivision. In other areas, wayfreight duties were normally handled by the through-freight crews although a wayfreight operated each way once a week over the Coquihalla and between Princeton and Midway. A locomotive was also assigned to move ore traffic from Copper Mountain to the concentrator at Allenby every day and then bring the concentrates to Princeton; two crews handled this assignment. South of Penticton a local service was operated three days a week but this was increased dramatically in the peak months of the fruit harvest. Work-train duties often kept three train crews busy across the division. The Penticton yards had an engine running or available 24 hours a day and three crews were assigned to this job. This was the situation on the Kettle Valley during the last years of steam operations and it was destined for rapid change.

The Kettle Valley relied on steam power until the early 1950s when the Canadian Pacific began the wholesale dieselization of its railway operations. All the characteristics that made the Kettle Valley a fascinating and charming, if rugged and brutal, railway contributed to its being an early candidate for the conversion from steam power to diesels and that story forms Part 3 of this book.

The following sections focus on the Kettle Valley during the height of the steam era: the equipment, its use on the railway, the day-to-day stories of living and working on the railway and the impressions of the engine and train crews, other railway employees, travellers and Kettle Valley families.

STEAM POWER, THE EARLY YEARS

The 3200s & the 500s—From 1916 through the 1920s, the Kettle Valley relied on the 3200 series 2-8-0s for most of its heavy assignments. They were used on passenger and freight trains and were tough, sturdy, hard-riding engines that had begun their years on the main line. They were classic steam power, of a type seen across North America from a turn-of-the-century generation of equipment that provided few comforts. Rugged, old unsophisticated "hogs," they were from an era when steam locomotives were still being developed and refined.

Sunlight filters through the back windows of the Penticton roundhouse to light several Kettle Valley locomotives including the 3120 in the foreground. This was where the KVR engines were serviced and cleaned and where running repairs were made. Heavy work was carried out at CPR facilities, often the large Ogden Shops at Calgary. —LUMB STOCKS PHOTO, HERITAGE PHOTO CO-OP

Returning from the First World War—Art Stiffe, water boy on the construction trains, returned from service during the First World War and signed on the KVR.

"We went down to the roundhouse at Penticton. They had those 3200 class locomotives that superseded the 3100s. We got on as wipers. Well, I had visions of wiping the rods and all around the locomotive. Instead they had the steam dome off this locomotive . . . and we were told to chip the scale off the inside of the boiler. 'Now you go up there, take your hammer and chisel, crawl down inside, work your way around the tubes in the shell of the boiler. . . .'

"Cold, damp, banging away on this scale on the boiler. We'd be in there for three and a half, four hours. Oh, and our ears! It was terrible. Well we did that for three or four days. This chum of mine had claustrophobia, oh he was scared. 'God, Art, I don't think I can stand it. I think I'm going to get trapped in there.' The last day, starting up he got scared and got his coat caught up near the top. 'Calm down, we'll get you up OK.' So I got his feet up and got him out. 'Never again, Art. I'm quitting.'

"I stayed on for a few days and I walked down to the shop one day looking for some waste and I made a mistake and asked Yeandle, the master mechanic, for some waste. 'You're supposed to go to the stockroom. You returned guys are all the same. You're fired.'"
—*Art Stiffe*, WIPER

"The little Kettle Valley 3200s in passenger service; somebody might get a chance to clean one up and maybe not. A lot depended on the master mechanic. If he had enough money in the reserve to spend more time cleaning engines, then more time was spent." —***W. Gibson Kennedy***

"The little 3200s had peanut whistles. The whistle sounded a high C and then, as the steam pressure would drop, it would drop in pitch a full tone to a B flat. The engineers all blew them differently. Charlie Craney, on freights, always had a special toot for his family." —***Glen Morley***

Musician and composer Glen Morley, inspired by memories of the Kettle Valley, wrote *Coquihalla Legends—A Railroad Rhapsody* for the Vancouver Youth Symphony Orchestra's 60th anniversary in 1990. It was recorded by the Orchestra, conducted and directed by Arthur Polson.

Classic Kettle Valley steam power from the 1920s at Calgary probably after being overhauled at the Ogden Shops. The 3224 was from the CPR's M2a class. It worked on the Kettle Valley in 1917-1921. The heavy wooden pilot is typical for engines on the KVR. —C. R. LITTLEBURY PHOTO, LANCE CAMP COLLECTION

Kettle Valley Railway Company

The 3250 at Iago on an eastbound train climbing the Coquihalla. This engine was one of the first 3200s on the Kettle Valley and worked passenger and freight assignments from May 1915 through July 1920. —BILL PRESLEY COLLECTION

Running and firing the old coal-burning "hogs" on the Kettle Valley was hard, dirty and noisy work but they were respected jobs of which to be proud. Engineer Sid Cornock and fireman, later engineer, Thomas Instone, both well known railwaymen, pose proudly in front of the 3280 at Penticton in the early 1920s. —DICK BROCCOLO COLLECTION

Firing the 3200s—"You had to have a lot of experience to fire them. It was quite a science. You'd stand out in that open deck and if you took a step back, you were off the engine. There was nothing to brace yourself on and every time you'd put coal on the fire, there was a chain on the door. You'd swing the door open and grab the scoop and hold the door. It was real hard. There were a few that were quite good steamers. But there was a lot of them that, oh boy, they were hard!" —*Burt Lye*, ENGINEER

Memories from along the Carmi Subdivision—"I remember being at Beaverdell in the late 1920s, watching the passenger train or riding from Beaverdell back to Trail and watching the fireman on those little wooden-cab 3200s. The boiler came right out to the end of the cab and there wasn't much room out there. The engineman couldn't see the fireman and vice versa because of the boiler. The fireman would sit on the windowsill of his side of the cab. It was cooler too, I guess, but that way, he could see the engineer over the boiler on the other side. It must have been hot in those little engines.

"At Beaverdell, I'd lie in bed at night and listen to the trains over at the station, just half a mile away. There would be two 3200s, one at the front end and a pusher at the tail end, and they'd whistle off with those single note whistles. The pusher man would give his two blasts to say 'we're ready to go' and when the engineman on the lead engine was given the signal to move off by the conductor, he'd blow too and away they'd go. I can hear those whistles still at night. They were going up to McCulloch, dropping the train and probably the pusher would come back to Midway and help another train; those fellows worked long hours."
—*W. Gibson Kennedy*

"Passenger trains must not exceed a speed of one mile in two minutes (30 miles per hour), and must not exceed a speed of one mile in two and one-half minutes (24 miles per hour) Coquihalla to Hope.

"Freight trains must not exceed a speed of one mile in four minutes (15 miles per hour) descending grade Coquihalla to Hope." —KETTLE VALLEY RAILWAY, TIMETABLE NO. 33, MAY 15, 1927

3200s and the Passenger Trains—"Before 1931, the passenger train was always four cars: a baggage and express; a day coach, either a 1200 or 1500 series; some of the 1500s had electric lights; and the 12-1 sleeper, with twelve sections and one drawing room; and the buffet-parlour-observation with the platform at the end. That car was rebuilt from an old coach-buffet years ago in Montreal. There were four of them assigned to the Kettle Valley, *Opinaka*, *Kettle*, *Similkameen*, and *Coquihalla*. Later they were given numbers 6521-6524. I used to watch those trains come and go.

"I can remember having a trip to Penticton in those wooden cars. You could almost see the cars twisting. They were wood construction: wooden-framed cars and beautifully done inside. I rode back in one car from Beaverdell. My aunt was a very generous person and while I had come from Trail to Beaverdell coach class, she got hold of the conductor, either Mr. McPherson or Mr. Thom, and asked him to upgrade my ticket to first class for the trip home. She bought a ticket for me in the buffet-parlour and I sat in there until the car was taken off at Farron. The car was removed from the end of the train at Farron, set in the siding there, and the next train, No. 11, going west, would pick up that car, observation platform leading, and take it to Midway where it was turned around on the wye so that the platform would be at the back for the trip to Penticton. —*W. Gibson Kennedy*

Winding its way through the Coquihalla in the early years of service, a 3200 leads a typical four-car passenger train westbound. —ARTHUR N. RISTON, GLENBOW ARCHIVES, NA4457-5

Too Many Bridges to Cross

The two huge trestles over the forks of Canyon Creek in Myra Canyon were replaced with steel bridges in 1932. After the Second World War, improvements included the 1947 reconstruction of the Bellevue Creek Bridge at Mile 96.3, shown at left. —PENTICTON MUSEUM, 37-4486

In the Coquihalla, a 3400 class 2-8-0, below, leads a train which includes a piledriver, eastbound over Ladner Creek bridge. At right, in 1951, a work train steams towards Coquihalla Summit. —BILL PRESLEY COLLECTION, BELOW; NICHOLAS MORANT, AT RIGHT

CANADIAN PACIFIC

HANDBOMBERS AND MCCULLOCH TURNS

The N2 class 2-8-0s, the 3600s, were the backbone of Kettle Valley Division steam power during the 1930s and 1940s. Tough and powerful, they were used on every assignment on the Kettle Valley. Nearly all were hand-fired coal burners for most of their years in Southern British Columbia. Two, and sometimes three, of these 1910-vintage engines were common on many Kettle Valley trains, particularly in Coquihalla Pass. A regular assignment was the McCulloch Turn for Penticton crews "working the east side."

Pausing for water, the *Kettle Valley Express* catches the morning sun in this beautiful photograph at Carmi. Standing on the step of the sleeping car on this August day in 1950 is Albert Anderson, roadmaster at Tadanac. —W. GIBSON KENNEDY

The 3600s Remembered—"I think the first 3600 came in 1932, after they strengthened the bridges. They had them working up the Coquihalla into Penticton. I don't know when they went east of Penticton. The first one I saw in Brookmere was 3688, the biggest engine I had ever seen, and the next one was the 3644 and then the 3684." —***Bill Presley***, BRAKEMAN

"There were some that we liked. The old 3663 was a crackerjack and the 3612 was a good engine, but the 3611 was no good at all. They changed them around; oh I guess 20, maybe 25, engines up there, 3600s. They'd put them through Ogden and maybe they'd never come back. We only had one 3500 and I think we only had one 3700 [more 3700s arrived in later years].

"Talk about strong ones, the 3623 and the 3624, they were [engineer] Hulett's favourites. They'd take the biggest train out of Brodie to Brookmere [over a one percent ascending grade eastbound], only four miles. We'd make a brief stop at Coquihalla and get the dispatcher to give us an order to pass Brodie without registering. We would come into Brodie and take a run at the hill to Brookmere, then we could wiggle in." —***Gordon Fulkerson***, ENGINEER

Steam on the Kettle Valley from the 1930s through the mid-1940s usually meant coal-fired, 3600 series, 2-8-0s such as the 3627 at Vancouver's Drake Street roundhouse on October 26, 1946. —WILBUR C. WHITTAKER COLLECTION

Weather-worn and scarred from years of hard service, the 3648, steams quietly at Midway probably before making a "turn" to McCulloch and back before returning to Penticton. Sometimes, crews made two turns to McCulloch before returning home to Penticton. They liked the mileage and the pay that went with it but long layovers with little to do were unpopular. Note the heavy wooden pilot, the smoke deflector on the stack and the coal bunker, piled high and ready for the fireman.
—TED WRIGHT

Frank Buttucci, Mac Wheeldon and Jack Nott, all logged many miles on the 3600s. —DICK BROCCOLO COLLECTION

"When you were called, there were about three questions you asked. 'What engine?' That would either make or break the trip. There were good engines and there were bum engines. Then the next question would be, 'Who's the hogger?' That could either make or break the trip. And one of the most important things, 'Who's the fireman?' So the odd time you'd get a good engine like the 3648, which I think was the best, and you'd get a good hogger and then to fill it out you'd get a good fireman; that really made the freight." —***Bill Presley***, BRAKEMAN

"Thirty-six hundreds, there were some good ones, some bad ones. The 3651 came in here from the prairies. It was somebody's private engine. I guess this guy just made a pet of that engine. He had it in just perfect shape. I remember going west one trip and back, and I got it to Midway and back with Rupy [Rupert] Johnson. Boy, what an engine! The valves were perfectly set, the rods were just perfect. Being that way, you get the perfect draft. Talk about steam. It was about the prettiest steaming engine I was ever on. It was by far the best 3600 I ever worked on. The 3650 was another real free-steaming engine." —***Burt Lye***, ENGINEER

Handfiring and Coal—"You put your fire in at the proper time, spread your coal pretty well evenly all over, especially in the back corners and down along the sides. You had to keep those two back corners really filled up or you couldn't keep her hot." —***Burt Lye***, ENGINEER

"A lot depended on what kind of coal you'd have. Comox coal was big lumps, and you used to carry your fire [a few inches] deep. You could clean a fire of Comox coal in no time at all, great big lumps. Middleboro or Coalmont coal, heck, your fire was 4 or 5 inches deep. The damn

Heavy canvas curtains, a warm coat, and a good hat provided little enough protection from the weather. —DICK BROCCOLO COLLECTION

Middlesboro coal was all slate, dirt and everything else. I've seen us stand there at Merritt after we came back from Nicola, clean our fire before we went on to Brookmere. . . . Then we'd stand there at the water tank and after we'd get the fire clean, by the time we get the steam back up, we'd have to start cleaning the fire again. Boy oh boy, they used to cuss us fellas, but you couldn't help it because it was so dirty. We used to go right up to the mine at Merritt and get our own coal right out of the chute.

"We used to have Michel coal, that was awful good. Fernie coal was awful fine. Comox coal, we only used to get that off CPR engines [working over the Kettle Valley] or when we'd coal up on the coast [at Ruby Creek] and work east through to Brookmere. We'd use it up on the hill [Coquihalla] as far as we could, and we'd save it. Take a little dirty coal at Brookmere, enough to take us down to Princeton, and then clean our fire down there, knock it down, and then shovel a little good Comox—you had to get up Jura Hill. Then once you got up Jura Hill, you were all right because it was pretty flat from there over to Osprey Lake. We tried to conserve and get all the Comox out of her we could." —*Gordon Fulkerson*, ENGINEER

"I had a pool job firing freight at Penticton in 1942. Thirty-six hundreds. If you went to Midway you got Michel coal at Carmi. With a half decent engine, it was a pretty good job. But if you went west you got a tank of that Bull Durham that they got out of those mines either at Coalmont or Merritt. That was some job. You were fighting all the way. Because you were young, you'd go with it. The preference job was the east side. You'd go over to Midway and often you'd make a McCulloch turn." —*Ernie Hawkes*, ENGINEER

"I was firing, coming up Jura Hill, 10 miles of 2.2 grade. It was a real nice sunny morning. All of a sudden, I think we had the 3612, this engine started to slip, and Johnny just couldn't get it stopped. I guess the sanders weren't working too good. So he went over to the right-of-way fence and cut a piece of wire and cleaned the sanders out. It just would not stop slipping. We slipped right to a stall. So I got off the engine and I looked up the track. You know what it was? On top of the rails was just one mass of grasshoppers. I guess they were sitting there getting the heat off the rails. The smell of those grasshoppers could just about knock you off your feet!" —*Burt Lye*, ENGINEER

Double-heading freights was an everyday occurrence on the Kettle Valley and three-engine trains were not uncommon. Two 3700s, with another engine at the rear, are smoking it up through Coquihalla. —DAVE WILKIE COLLECTION

McCulloch Turns—"We'd go over to Midway and sometimes we'd made one McCulloch turn; first we'd go east, book rest, and then get called and work to McCulloch and back. Then we'd get another trip, west from Midway. We'd couple the two trains together coming up the next day at McCulloch and then bring them over the hump and into Penticton. When you went over that hump, if you were going four or five miles an hour, you were doing pretty good.

"From Midway to McCulloch, you'd have 1,300 tons. You'd come into Penticton with 2,600 tons. That was quite a chore, bringing a train down from Chute Lake. There were an awful lot of straight stretches coming down from Chute Lake and it took more controlling than it would coming down the Coquihalla where you have so many twists and turns.

"When I was firing, it was a challenge with some engines, and a poor tank of coal. Lots of times, when I got off those engines to walk over to the bunk house I was so tired I could hardly make it. You get a poor engineer, some guy that would put it right down in the corner and really go after it. It made an awful difference who your engineer was." —***Burt Lye***, ENGINEER

Midway was the turnaround point for Penticton crews and from where they would make a McCulloch turn. The 3644 has brought a freight in from Penticton and, at right, the 5204, a recently rebuilt 2-8-2, is awaiting the next call in this scene from the late 1940s. —TED WRIGHT

Storming eastbound out of Penticton, double-headed 2-8-2s have their train rolling with 27 miles (43.5 km) of ascending 2.2 percent grade ahead. —RAY MATTHEWS

—ROBERT D. TURNER

The remote community of Carmi could be busy. At left, a short westbound freight behind the 3609 steams away towards McCulloch. The caboose had developed a hotbox, necessitating a 15-minute stop to change the brass bearing. Below left, the crew has topped up the coal in 5230's tender for the run to Penticton while below, another freight, gathering speed, passes the station. —W. GIBSON KENNEDY

"Crews may be required to make two short turn-around trips out of a terminal, with the understanding that a crew shall not be started out . . . on a second turn-around trip after having been on duty eight hours or more." —*Schedule of Rates of Pay, Rules and Working Conditions for Conductors, Brakemen and Flagmen*, 1922

"The minute you went to work you got 100 miles, whether 5 minutes' work, you got your 100 miles. In freight service, you would be paid initial terminal time and final terminal time. So if you were called for a McCulloch turn, you'd be paid 12.5 cents a mile for terminal time if you're switching. The minute you left the outer main track switch, you'd go onto road miles; nearly 135 miles to Midway. You'd also get paid final terminal delay, putting your train away at Midway. Then you might be called for a McCulloch turn. So you'd get initial terminal time at Midway, then you'd go to McCulloch, roughly 75 miles. You'd set out your turn then go back, caboose hop, to Midway, where you'd be paid your road miles . . . and final terminal time at Midway. And you'd also get paid turnaround time at McCulloch, 12.5 miles [for each] hour. If you had a couple of hours' switching a Midway, that's 25 miles. You could get 175-180 miles for a turn there." —***Bill Presley***, BRAKEMAN

"These fellows all liked McCulloch turns because it was pretty good miles. By the time you made the running miles and the McCulloch turns, it made a pretty good deal out of it." —***Ernie Hawkes***, ENGINEER

Angus Gillis looks ready to demolish his unsuspecting friend on the steps of a typical, well-worn bunkcar.
—DICK BROCCOLO COLLECTION

Bunkhouses—Nearly all work on the railway meant spending some time living in bunkhouses, or for the train crews, the cabooses. At the end of a trip from Penticton to Brookmere, Brookmere to Ruby Creek, or from Penticton to Midway, the crews had time off, "booked rest," and could eat and catch some sleep. For men on the McCulloch turns, for example, a lot of time could be spent in the Midway bunkhouse between turns and trips home. Section crews also lived in company bunkhouses and gangs on work trains often spent weeks at a time in bunkcars. Crews often had little privacy in the bunkhouses and boredom during long layover periods could be a problem. Card games sometimes became marathons and visits to the local hotel beer parlour could be a temptation. Conditions in these facilities improved slowly over the years and they were one focus for continuing pressure from the unions for improvements.

"Our bunkhouses were very, very poor on the Kettle Valley, but the job was so tough. . . . I can remember the steam days, you went right into that bed, you didn't care; you were so tired, you went there to sleep. Naturally it wasn't too sanitary at times. At Brookmere, they used to hire somebody to clean it up. The same at Midway. We packed all our own grub in our own boxes to cook up over there ourselves. What I took lasted me for three days. [In the early days] we never even had fridges. All these things were fought about and eventually you got them improved.

"They'd tell you you were set up on a work train to go over to Myra Canyon for 10 days. And there's an outfit car, with a couple of pails and a few dirty old frying pans. You have to take your 10 days' grub over there with you. So you talk it over with the train crews and everybody figures out who's going to be the cook. . . . whatever the guys ahead of us had, they were happy with it, but you get a bunch of younger ones in there and they build it up a little more." —***Dick Broccolo***, ENGINEER

"I collared the master mechanic at Brookmere. I said, 'These sheets should be changed more than once a month.' He took a look at them and said, 'I don't see much to complain about. They look about as good as what I sleep in at home.' So I said, 'Don't say that out loud.' But he wouldn't change those sheets. When I was wiping at Brookmere, I'd change those sheets religiously once a week. I'd send an order into Nelson where they had a laundry. Even though some of those guys did jump into bed with their clothes on after shovelling coal all day." —*Ernie Hawkes*, ENGINEER

"My dad, Bob Hansen, didn't like living in bunkhouses so he built himself a little cabin at Hope on the banks of the Fraser River and when he was building this we used to go down quite a lot and help. We'd have fun going and picking berries and that sort of thing. It was a real outing because we could travel for nothing. The bunkhouse was too noisy, people would want to play cards or talk and he had trouble sleeping. He also built cottages at Midway and Brookmere." —*Ruth Hansen McGregor*

Ernie Hawkes beside the bunkhouse at Princeton. Between trips it was laundry time. —ERNIE HAWKES COLLECTION

Brookmere railroaders, left to right, Angus Gillis, Gerry Smuin, Bob Barwick, unknown, Jack Vader, Bill Osborne, Murdoch MacKay, Cyril Hawkins, unknown, Tom Clarke. Below, Jim Barnes, brakeman, outside the Brookmere bunkhouse in 1949. —DICK BROCCOLO COLLECTION; JIM BARNES COLLECTION

Merritt normally was served by a mixed train from Brookmere, but when the Coquihalla was closed, the *Kootenay Express* and the *Kettle Valley Express* were detoured through town. Such was the case on this day in the 1920s when the passenger train stopped at the water tank.
—BILL PRESLEY COLLECTION

"In the spring, I used to ship out ten carloads of cattle every Monday morning [from Nicola]. That was just from one outfit, the Douglas Lake Cattle Company. They were shipping them to Vancouver; P. Burns and Swift Canadian were the big buyers. . . . There was no passenger business to speak of; just a mixed train. . . . It was an old man's job as far as that went, but the wages were good. I weighed all the cattle." —***Reid Johnston***, STATION AGENT AT NICOLA, 1917-1924

"When they were coming or going to or from Spences Bridge from Merritt, there were all these cattle around. Of course they were dodging them all the time. One did get near the train and they stopped and the brakeman chased it away, not knowing that one had been caught on the cowcatcher. Harry looked around and couldn't see that cow anywhere. So they started out again and went within a few miles of Merritt and they stopped to check and there was that cow on the cowcatcher. Harry thought she was dead, but she got up and ran off." —***Til Percival***, RECALLING ONE OF HARRY PERCIVAL'S FAVOURITE STORIES

Merritt, situated in a broad, dry valley shadowed by the mountains to the west, became an important centre on the Kettle Valley. Its economy developed around coal mining, noteably the Middlesboro Colliery, ranching and sawmilling. The trackage from Spences Bridge through Merritt to Brookmere was progressively improved as detours of traffic from the Coquihalla became all too predictible. The generally level line through the Nicola Valley was a marked contrast to the mountainous nature of most sections of the Kettle Valley. Crews from Brookmere handled traffic to Spences Bridge and a two- or three-times a week mixed train, "The Jitney," provided the passenger service. During the 1930s and 1940s a once-a-week mixed train also ran between Brookmere and Hope.

"They'd get the 'Jitney,' the mixed train to Merritt. There was absolutely nothing for people in Brookmere. That went out from Monday to Saturday. Harry and Burt Josephson were on it. . . . They'd be called earlier, 1 a.m. or 2 for 4 [o'clock]. They were terrible hours. They used to groan and moan about it because it was a small engine, a 3400, instead of a 36. It was smaller pay and it was nothing but switching at Merritt, at the mills. Then they'd go to Upper Nicola to load cattle all day. Believe me, by the time they'd get back to Merritt and to Spences Bridge, they'd be just played out. That was a tough trip and the wages were smaller." —***Til Percival***

BROOKMERE

Brookmere, on the east side of the Cascade Mountains, was once one of the most important points, from an operational perspective, on the Kettle Valley Railway. Brookmere became the divisional point between the Kettle Valley's Coquihalla and Princeton subdivisions and also the terminal from which crews on the "Jitney" ran over the Merritt Subdivision from Brodie to Spences Bridge.

Brookmere was the base for pusher crews, freight and passenger-train crews, and snowplow trains. Crews working west and to Merritt and Spences Bridge lived there while those based at Penticton who worked the trains to and from Brookmere "booked rest" and had layover periods before returning east. Engines were serviced there, taking on fuel, water and sand. Fires were cleaned, running gear was lubricated. Passenger trains ran through in both directions on a daily basis and freights toiled through the small town with the cars of concentrates, produce, lumber and other commodities.

"Brookmere was never anything but a mountain railway terminal consisting of maybe 20 family dwellings, the hotel, store, post office and a small school house," recalled Perley McPherson, KVR conductor. The Kettle Valley Railway was its reason for being. The 1936 *British Columbia Directory* gave the population as 125 and of those listed five out of six worked on the Kettle Valley. Few people came to Brookmere to make it a permanent home, especially after a few bad winters.

With the dieselization of the railway and subsequent changes in operating patterns, Brookmere declined. The construction of the Trans Mountain pipeline brought some activity and maintenance staff were assigned there. However, after the dismantling of the Kettle Valley and the construction of the Coquihalla Highway which bypassed the community, it remained the home of only a few residents, often retired, and of some people with summer cottages. Few people travelling through would guess how busy a place this all-but-forgotten spot had been during the Kettle Valley's steam era.

"I arrived in Brookmere in 1920. My dad [Frank Presley] was agent there from 1920 until about 1943. I went to school in the one-room schoolhouse. I was about 15½ when I started work on the section. I worked for a while on an extra gang and then started with the communications department and worked in the Coquihalla in the winter climbing poles and looking after the communications. I spent quite a bit of time in Romeo and then in the summer, worked on bridge and building gangs; that went on for several years until 1936 when I got an opportunity to go braking.

"I was the first brakeman hired in six years. We were just coming out of the Depression. So the fellow ahead of me was a 1930 man and I came in seniority from 1936. I bucked the spare board for seven long years and eventually got on the steady crew.

Brookmere scenes: the enginehouse before a boiler explosion nearly destroyed the building; the 3628 near the ash pit with the combination car used on the Jitney at right; and a day in the winter of 1956. Brookmere's water tower, section house and a caboose have been preserved—the section house as a private museum by Harry Fontaine.
—RUTH HANSEN MCGREGOR COLLECTION; MAC WHEELDON PHOTOS, DICK BROCCOLO COLLECTION

"In 1942, the Japanese people were sent through and some of them were here. We had Little Tokyo, two rows of new little places. . . . I remember standing out in the porch, and they stopped right in front of our place. There were six to eight big long coaches. In some of them were Japanese people on stretchers or in beds, and there were RCMP on each end, guarding. These people all looked so sad. They would be out there for a few hours, waiting for another engine to get ready to take them. They were going to Greenwood and other places where there were internment camps." —*Til Percival*

"Brookmere folded up after they closed the Coquihalla because there were no crews coming down there. Then they started running the wayfreight between Penticton and Spences Bridge and it went right through Brookmere. Down one day and back the next. The odd day they'd run up to Nicola and pick up a little stock there."
—*Gordon Fulkerson*, ENGINEER

"In my time, they didn't have the community hall. If there was any function, there was a fairly good-sized schoolhouse they'd use. Outside of the postmaster, the teacher, a trapper or two, a woodcutter or two, a storekeeper there were just the railroad crews and families."
—*Bill Presley*, BRAKEMAN

"We lived next to the coal chute. What do you think of that? They put a passing track in right in front of our porch. I could hand the bucket out to Harry just as he was going by; that's how close. I got used to all that in a short time. But anyone visiting us, they thought it was terrible. They thought the whole place was coming down when they were switching or anything.

"This was a busy place. We had the passengers coming in every night. First we had No. 11 and 12 and then 45 and 46. Harry was on that for a couple of years. I'd get on it many times and go to Penticton with him. We'd visit at his mum's and get back on it next evening. Made a nice little trip. I liked it, it was fast.

"I was a loner. I came from a little town in Saskatchewan and coming up here was fine. Soon as Harry would get home, I'd pack more sandwiches. We'd hike through all the hills. Nobody had a car. We used our trains. If we wanted to go to Vancouver for the day, which was very convenient, we got on during the night and got into Vancouver at 8 or 9 a.m. and had all day until 7:30 or 8 to shop. That's the way we did things.

"We used to have some dances here in Brookmere in June. Everyone had a hand in building the community hall. It was opened in June of 1946. It was a big do! We had CPR officials here to open it. From then on we had June dances every year. There were some great ones. Talk about fights and everything. Sometimes, they'd go to Merritt with a coach and bring people from Merritt or Princeton. Some would come from Penticton. It was very formal at first, but it got to be quite informal later. You had your gowns and the men were all dressed up. It was really nice. But I would say sometimes a drunken affair." —*Til Percival*

"In the wintertime, the boys used to fix up a skating rink there; take the engine out and flood a little piece of ice beside the track. They got old bridge timbers and built a community hall. We had dances there and gatherings. The superintendent said sure if the bridge men would bring them in and build it. We used to have a lot of fun at those Saturday night dances. We had a picnic there at the school and we had a ball team." —*Gordon and Audrey Fulkerson*

"The phone rang and by 21 o'clock, 'Deadhead to Brookmere on No. 11.' Well I figured we were going to Brookmere on an engine. Sometimes they'd deadhead a crew to pick up an engine after repairs in Vancouver. So anyway I get down to the shop and I says 'Where's the hoghead?' 'Oh, you haven't got an engineer, You're going to Brookmere hostling.'* I could have quit right then. We'd just settled down in Penticton and they sent me to Brookmere. 'You should be there about a month.'

"Dead of winter, I get off that train at Brookmere, and I can see that snow yet, it was piled up over the top of the station. This is Brookmere. I stayed in the bunkhouse, didn't work that night because it was after midnight. No food or lunch bucket. I didn't bring anything."
—*Ernie Hawkes*, ENGINEER

* A hostler's job was to move engines around the terminal and prepare them for the engine crews coming on duty.

Athena "Beca" Apostoli grew up in the Kettle Valley section house at Tulameen about one hour west of Princeton by train. Her father, Alexander Cappos, was section foreman, and her uncle was section foreman at Manning. Before moving to Tulameen, the family lived at Jura to the east of Princeton. Life in the isolated communities along the railway provided few amenities and, in the smallest railway locations, little or no social life. The work of maintaining the right-of-way, was hard and hours were long. Some families found the life satisfying and happy but others found the isolation oppressive and too much to bear.

The Cappos family and some other Kettle Valley people came from Greece; others working on the sections came from Italy, the Ukraine, Yugoslavia, China, Portugal and many other countries.

"My father, Alexander Cappos, was 16 when he came out, 85 years ago, in 1910. He was in New York and then Chicago and then heard about the railway being built and needing men; that there was lots of work here. So he threw all his clothing in a trunk—even his unwashed socks—[and left]. There was no trouble with the border at all. They just opened the trunk and closed it again.

"He worked on the gang they had that travelled doing the buildings while they were building the railway. They had a Chinese cook for the gang and my father taught him Greek cooking, all the Greek dishes that he remembered watching his mother cook. Sundays especially, when he didn't have to feed the whole camp, he would cook the dinner for several of the Greeks who were on the gang.

"My mother's father, Louis Drosses, was a section foremen at Belfort. And that's where mum and dad met. One at Jura and one at Belfort. We often teased them and said, 'Oh they met on a speeder. My father had an accident on the speeder, real bad one. Mum was on one speeder and dad was on the other. They collided!'

"After they were married they went to Tulameen from Jura. They got a railway car and put all their chickens, a cow and I think they had a sheep, in the boxcar and took them to Tulameen.

"My father's brother, Tom, brought his wife-to-be from Greece. He was the section foreman at Manning. Manning was the next section from Tulameen. The wedding was held here in Tulameen and people came from all over. They even brought the priest from Seattle because there was no Greek Orthodox priest in Vancouver then. The wedding went on for three days and three nights. My mother still remembers it because she did the cooking for the group. There were so many people, they slept in the station; they had approval. They partied, they danced, they had their music, their Greek dancing. So it was a real ethnic wedding.

"My mother remembers, holding the baby all in white. Oh, she says, 'that was Frances, we baptized her that day. . . . The priest was there, so we baptised her because he'd come for the wedding.'" —*Athena Apostoli*

The isolation on the remote sections of the Kettle could be a difficult adjustment. Often, there was just the section foreman and family, the section crew and perhaps a telegraph operator and, except for the passing trains, no social life at all.

BELFORT, JURA AND TULAMEEN

"I can remember a stormy night sitting there, waking up and worrying, in case there was a slide and he would have to get called in. When there were slides in the Coquihalla, they all used to have to go and stay there until the slides were cleared. We wouldn't know when he would come back; sometimes he'd be gone three days, three nights until they'd cleared the slides. He was worried about his own section too." —*Athena Apostoli*

The small section house at Belfort where Louis Drosses was section foreman. The Drosseses' daughter Kalomera, "Karla," met and married Alexander Cappos, foreman at Jura, the next section to the east. —CAPPOS FAMILY COLLECTION

Family and friends gathered at Tulameen in 1925 for the wedding of Tom and Pauline Cappos and the christening of Frances Cappos.
—CAPPOS FAMILY COLLECTION

Alexander Cappos, about 1958, in front of the Tulameen section house that was the family home. In an earlier photo Athena "Beca" Cappos, Gladys Forsyth, Ruth Sootheran, Frances Cappos and John Cappos stand in the tracks before school.
—CAPPOS FAMILY COLLECTION

"My mother's family went back to Greece and she had the choice of going back or staying and marrying father, which she did. So many went back. My father's brother went back too, took the family. The children were born here and they went back. It was mostly the women that couldn't tolerate being out in the country with nobody around. Especially at Manning. At least at Tulameen you had school and there was a bit of a community there. But I think it was very hard on the women. Very isolated.

"What I found too was the way they adapted, food-wise, culture-wise. They had to adapt quickly. I can remember my mum canning meat and making Greek stews. She made their own Feta cheese. You could never get that. The Italian store was in Vancouver, and you could get olive oil and olives from them and Parmesan cheese, but no Feta cheese.

"We had a beautiful garden in the summer. Mum used to grow her own spinach and make her own spinach pies. We had a root cellar too that the company built, in concrete, right under our kitchen, with bins in it. We kept carrots there all winter and the potatoes and cabbages kept well. We could go to Princeton and do a big shopping. In the winters when the road was closed, my father would order from Woodward's [in Vancouver], especially around Christmas time, when he wanted his seafood. Woodward's would pack up a great big crate of prawns and crabs and send them on the train. In a few hours, over Coquihalla to Tulameen, we had our fresh seafood, all on ice. In later years, the butcher in Princeton used to deliver meat to the train and my father would have it in three-quarters of an hour, an hour. That was personal service.

"He took a big pride in his section. And he was very conscientious. He had a very good name. He had the smoothest line of anyone on the Kettle Valley, that is what they told him."
—Athena Apostoli

The mark of a good section foreman was immaculate trackage. As Beca Apostoli (née Cappos) recalled, "My father didn't leave a weed growing anywhere. . . . He got his crew working and there wasn't one weed left. And the section house would always be clean, neat and tidy."
—CAPPOS FAMILY COLLECTION

COPPER MOUNTAIN

The Copper Mountain Subdivision, just 13.6 miles (21.8 km) long, between Princeton and Copper Mountain, was the shortest subdivision but at the same time one of the most important revenue sources for the entire railway. Built between 1918 and 1920, this branch line's sole purpose was to serve the copper mining operations of Canadian Copper Corporation (acquired in 1920 by the Granby Consolidated Mining, Smelting & Power Co.). Construction was delayed by the 1918 influenza epidemic which hit the contractors and then in April 1919 by a strike. The line had hardly been completed and the first ore shipments handled about November 1, 1920, when the mine was closed indefinitely at the end of December. The branch line suffered heavy cost overruns with the total price coming in at nearly double the 1917 estimates. In the end it cost over $150,000 a mile (over $90,000 a km) or a total of about $2,200,000, much to the chagrin of senior CPR management.

"That was an interesting little piece of railroad. Lots of rockslides would come down. It was a bad spot but then again it was very slow traffic. We never went more than 10 or 12 miles an hour. . . . You were under retainers coming down with the loads and going up you were hauling your tonnage [empty cars] so you could stop. It was relatively safe."
—*Dick Broccolo*, ENGINEER

In July 1923 the tracks were repaired and made ready for operations but the opening of the mine was once again delayed and the railway was not reopened until August 20, 1925. Over the years, the demand for copper varied greatly and with the Depression, mining was suspended. Between December 5, 1930, and May 16, 1937, the subdivision was closed. Reopened in 1937 at a cost of $70,000, the branch remained in operation for 20 years.

During the late 1940s, three or four ore trains a day usually operated between the mine at Copper Mountain and the concentrator at Allenby, 5.8 miles (9.4 km) from Princeton. The daily production of about 5,000 tons (4 535 tonnes) of ore was processed, yielding about three cars of concentrates a day which were shipped to Tacoma, Washington, for smelting. The Copper Mountain Subdivision remained active until the mine shut down in April 1957. Nearly all the trackage soon was removed. The community of Copper Mountain was eventually demolished and the site consumed by open-pit mining after the demise of the railway. Ore from this operation was removed by aerial tramway.

Princeton was the base for the Copper Mountain crews. In the Princeton yards, the 3676, with loads of concentrates from Allenby, meets a westbound extra in 1950. —W. GIBSON KENNEDY

"The Copper Mountain job was a separate issue altogether from the pusher crew at Princeton. There were two crews, a day job and a night job. In my time, old Jimmy Carmichael was on the day job and Billy Roberts was on the night job. The day job went to work at 7:00 o'clock in the morning and he usually got tied up around 18 o'clock at night. Then the next job would be called 20:30 or 21 o'clock. He'd use the same engine, 3627. I had the 3629, a hand-fired coal-burner, boy it was a good steamer. The train crew slept in the caboose and there was a little bit of a bunkhouse . . . about the size of this kitchen, a bed and a stove [for the engine crew]."
—*Ernie Hawkes*, ENGINEER

A train loading ore at Copper Mountain and soon to ease down the grade to the concentrator at Allenby near Princeton.
—BILL PRESLEY

"It was always a 12-hour shift, seven days a week until you couldn't stand it any more. Going up to Allenby we had 50-foot gondolas for the concentrates. We'd pick up the ore cars at Allenby and go up to Copper Mountain and load the crushed ore. We'd take those down to Allenby and dump them. That was a 2 percent grade and we had to use the retainers. We'd make two trips then pick up any of the large gondolas, to go to a smelter, then we'd go back to Princeton."
—***Jim Barnes***, BRAKEMAN

At Allenby, trainmen Bill Presley and Tom McLellan pose beside the 3506. Engineer Tom McAstocker is leaning out of the cab window next to Bob Blacklock, fireman.
—BILL PRESLEY

Beneath dark and threatening skies, the crew prepares to ease the 3687 onto the turntable at Copper Mountain.
—BILL PRESLEY

3687
3687

The benchlands and dry valley bottom of the southern Okanagan had the potential to produce some of the finest fruit grown in Canada. Several decades of work were needed to bring the dreams of the early promoters and farmers to reality. Orchards had to mature, irrigation had to be established, packing and transportation systems had to be built and markets developed. In the southern Okanagan, the communities of Summerland and Naramata on the shore of Okanagan Lake prospered. Penticton became a prime fruit growing area with the orchards extending south from Okanagan Lake to Dog, or Skaha, Lake.

In 1920 the expanding opportunities for agricultural development in the southern Okanagan prompted construction of a spur line from the yards at Penticton to Skaha Lake. The steamer *York*, transferred to Skaha from Okanagan Lake, and a small railcar barge began a service south to Okanagan Falls. From there, tracks were laid to Haynes, 3.4 miles (5.5 km) south of Oliver and, by 1923, regular service began over what became known as the Osoyoos Subdivision. Shippers could load fruit directly onto railcars and move it up the valley by rail and water to Penticton. In 1931, the Skaha Lake barge service was eliminated by the construction of trackage along the shore. The final extension of trackage south to Osoyoos was completed in 1944.

Peaches, apples, plums and pears became key crops as the orchards matured. Cantaloupe and zucca melons also were important. The latter, a tasteless fruit, was used as a base for preserves. So important did cantaloupe production become that trains, known informally at least as "Cantaloupe Specials," ran up the valley from the Oliver area to Penticton.

By the mid-1920s, the post-First World War economic slump and many of the problems of adjusting to peacetime conditions had passed. In the Okanagan, the fruit growing industry had matured and prime products were being shipped across the country. Fresh, perishable fruit was often shipped by Dominion Express in cars usually included in the passenger trains. Long trains of ice refrigerator cars, being hastened to the main line, symbolized the fruit season.

West Summerland recollections—"The big Cooperative was down at the lower town, Summerland. Both CPR and the CNR were there [on the lakeshore]. I never got any carloads of fruit because I was too far away from the packing houses. They could take the loads down the hill to the lake instead of bringing them up. They went out on the barge service. There was a separate agency down there. I was mostly handling passenger traffic—tickets, l.c.l. [less-than-carload lots] freight, small stuff. Gosh I worked hard there."
—***Reid Johnston***, WEST SUMMERLAND STATION AGENT, 1926-1952

"We used to watch the girls peeling zucca melons as we were going south in the early days. They'd be out on the platform of the packing house with draw knives, just like woodworking draw knives, and they were peeling the damn things."
—***Alan Palm***, CONDUCTOR

Reid Johnston, who later was for many years station agent at West Summerland, left, and J. H. "Hi" Henry at Beaverdell in 1916. The Carmi mail sack is on the ground beside the train. At that time, the passenger train had just three cars: a baggage-coach, a day coach and a sleeper.
—BILL PRESLEY COLLECTION

The trains to Oliver, in the early days, often drew older power not suited to the grades of the Kettle Valley main line. The 3092 worked the branch in the early 1920s and was followed by the 3090.
—BILL PRESLEY COLLECTION

"On the branch down to Osoyoos, a lot of fruit came out even in cattle cars. They went to the canneries and jam factories. That was some of the best eating fruit; you could reach through the slats and get peaches and they were really ripe. They would ship the various melons as well in the cattle cars. They were cleaned up of course. Water melons, zucca melons, stacked in there. They loaded them in just like cordwood." —*Jim Barnes*, BRAKEMAN

South to Oliver and Osoyoos—"An old hoghead named Otis [Otinus] Ruud, in 1926 or '27, said to me, 'It looks like I'm going to get the south in the morning. Would you like to go?' Would I like to go! 'Oh goodness yes, I sure would like to go.' So we go down to the shop track and he says to keep out of the way. On the shop track sat the 3090. It had a whistle that was right in front of the window with no shield or anything on it. When he blew that whistle, everything came in the cab.

"After we have our brake test and are all set up, away we go for Oliver. We get down to the north end of Skaha and the barge is there. He'll accommodate the engine, caboose and two cars. He had a steam tug [the *York*], and loaded the outfit on the barge. We get down to Okanagan Falls and get off again. It was quite a performance to get this thing all organized but nobody was in a hurry.

"They get down to Oliver and spot up the cars. The brakemen are busy loading the caboose; I've never seen so much fruit. The guy comes out and he says, 'Listen, fellas, I don't mind you taking the culls, but that's all overseas.' About 18 o'clock, it's about time to head back home. We get these two reefers and the caboose and . . . back to Okanagan Falls. The barge is on this end of the lake and we take it back and go back into Penticton. We get tied up on the shop track about 21 o'clock." —*Ernie Hawkes*, ENGINEER, RECALLING HIS FIRST TRIP SOUTH OF PENTICTON BEFORE HE STARTED WIPING

"Everything had gone at midnight, so you knew you were going to get the south in the morning if you were first out. You'd get called for the 588. . . . We'd have four reefers and a caboose. In Oliver, we spot up the reefers, that's it for the day. They hadn't built to Osoyoos yet. So we just sat around all day and when time came to go we gathered up the cars, took off and went back to Penticton."
—*Ernie Hawkes*, ENGINEER

"You went down as far as Haynes below Oliver. It was just a freight to switch the packing houses. You'd take a few empty cars down, reefers or stock cars, and bring them back. There was a great run of zucca melons. The stock cars were open, ventilated, and they'd clean them out. Mostly, it was end-bunker ice reefers. Cantaloupe would come to Penticton and then be barged to Kelowna. Not a great deal, as I recall, went west out of Penticton. I remember the odd train with five or six reefers, but the bulk of it went up the lake. Not very much went east."
—*Bill Presley*, TRAINMAN

"The track to Osoyoos [from Haynes] was built during the war with Japanese labour. That was when they were moved from the coast. No Orientals were allowed here in Oliver or Osoyoos. They got orders they had to stay on company property. Anybody got sick, I'd have to chaperon them to the doctor's office. They lived in camps. They had outfit cars and down here, about four miles, they set up a big shower, with steambaths, because they liked their steambaths. A wooden frame around outside where they camped. They worked from there to Osoyoos, building the railway." —***Albert Martino***, MACHINERY OPERATOR

Satisfied Customers—There was sometimes a state of simmering hostility between the railway and the fruit growers in the Okanagan. The availability of freight cars, particularly refrigerator cars for fruit, was always a bone of contention leading to this story, probably apocryphal:

"One year as the warm days of summer passed, the peach crop was looking perfect but when it came time to ship the crop, there was a shortage of refrigerator cars and not all of the fruit could be handled. Harsh words were recalled vividly by the station agent.

"The next year the crop was poor but an abundant supply of refrigerator cars was available. The grower looked at the empty cars by the packing house and shook his head in despair.

"Then came a year in the Okanagan when everything looked perfect. The crop came in as a bumper harvest, there were refrigerator cars waiting at the packing house and all was well. The peaches, large and succulent were close to perfection. Picking was to begin the next morning. Then, before dawn, a violent hailstorm struck the district. At first light, the grower went out onto his verandah. A faint mist was rising but, as he looked out over his orchard, he could see that his crop had been devastated. He raised his eyes to the sky and shook his fist with all the fury he could muster and shouted, 'God damn the CPR!'"
—TOLD TO PETER CORLEY-SMITH BY A CPR OFFICIAL IN PENTICTON, 1975

The Oliver Station, in the 1970s. It became a community centre. The Osoyoos station, also preserved, is very similar. —ROBERT A. LOAT

West Summerland, a few miles from Summerland, was as close as the KVR came to the town but it was still a busy station. Most fruit was shipped out by tug and barge or sternwheeler from the lakeshore. The station was stuccoed in its later years, as shown at right. The building was a community museum before being demolished. —SUMMERLAND MUSEUM

Vancouver was the destination of many travellers over the Kettle Valley, an important market for the Okanagan's fruit and also as the main merchandise supplier for many communities. In 1947, Trains 45 and 46 were added to the service between Vancouver and Penticton. In February 1949, the 5121 on Train No. 45 steams along the shore of Burrard Inlet with nine cars heading to Vancouver.
—ANDRE MORIN

Fast Service to the Coast—"After they got the big trucks, they could load them up [with fruit] and put them in Vancouver quicker than we did with the train. That was what 45 and 46 went on for, an extra fast train. The 11 and 12 were true passenger trains that went on right through the Crow.

"Train 46 started at Penticton and went to Vancouver. Left there about 8:00 at night with the fruit brought up from the Oliver district in iced-reefers, and a passenger car, sometimes just a combination car, on the end. We'd try to get it into Vancouver by 9:00 the next morning.

"I worked 45 and 46 out of Vancouver. We used to go up on 46 and come back on 11 and go up on 12 and come back on 45. There was only about 4 or 5 hours layover between trains at the time. They had diesels on the 11 and 12, but they had steampots on the 45 and 46 because they only had a light train. We used to handle the mail too, instead of having to stop 11 and 12, which were big long trains. Coming down, we'd maybe have 5 or 6 cars of cherries, trying to get them into market." —*Gordon Fulkerson*, ENGINEER

The Coquihalla Subdivision of the Kettle Valley was one of the toughest stretches of railroad in the western mountains. The combination of steep grades, a twisting, turning route, enormous snowfalls and heavy rain made it a constant challenge for both the operating and maintenance crews. Rockfalls, slides and washouts were hazards that could never be far from the minds the crews. Repairing the yearly cycle of damage was a never-ending battle.

In other, similar situations where railroads crossed high passes with heavy snow, tunnelling and line relocations usually solved the problem. The original Canadian Pacific main line over Rogers Pass was eliminated at the time of the Coquihalla's opening by the completion of the Connaught Tunnel. To the south in the Cascades, the Great Northern eliminated its first and second routes over Stevens Pass by its famous Cascade tunnels.

Traffic on the Coquihalla did not justify the investment required for such massive projects. Some years were worse than others but the winter of 1931-32 illustrates the extent of the problems and damage that could befall the Coquihalla route. By early March 1932, between Coquihalla station and Petain, reports recorded over 60 slides, washouts, rockfalls or areas of damage to the railway. Estimates for 17 of the slides placed the amount of material over the tracks at nearly 12,000 cubic yards (over 10,000 m^3). Twelve more slides covered over 1,800 feet (nearly 550 m) of track in depths up to 18 feet (5.5 m). In addition, bridges, retaining walls and snowsheds were damaged or destroyed. Sixteen stretches of track, totalling nearly 1,700 feet (520 m), were washed out.

Each spring the cleanup and repair crews went back to work and reopened the line but there was never any assurance that the hard labour would not be undone by the next winter. As if in counterpoint, the summers sometimes held the threat of forest fires. In 1938 fires west of the summit destroyed three major bridges closing the line for two months and at the same time increased the wintertime slide danger by removing the forest cover. Probably the only positive side was that there was no shortage of work for railroaders and contractors in the Coquihalla.

Train handling required special skill, care and attention on mountain grades and the descent from Coquihalla to Hope was governed by strict procedures. The train crews were professionals and knew the hazards of operating in the mountains and the reasons behind the regulations. The remarkable safety record of Coquihalla trains underlines how conscientious and skilled the men were.

"God, coming up there in the winter time—some of those snow slides! They should have had a snowshed right from Coquihalla to Hope." —*Burt Lye*, ENGINEER

At Romeo, the *Kootenay Express* meets the *Kettle Valley Express* on July 4, 1952. Clouds are rolling in from the Pacific and there will be rain before the day is over.
—JOHN ILLMAN

An eastbound freight behind a 3600 has the fireman working hard as it rounds the curved bridge over Ladner Creek.
—MAC WHEELDON,
DICK BROCCOLO COLLECTION

"Going up the Coquihalla, it used to be pretty grim through the snowsheds. No. 11 and 12 sheds were both 1,400 feet long and you had to put in a fire when you were going through the sheds. It was pretty hard to get a breath of fresh air under those conditions. . . . When there were three engines on a train, there'd be two on the headend and one ahead of the caboose. If you were on that second engine, the exhaust would be hitting the roof of the shed and coming down on that second engine. Most engines had an elbow on the stack but others didn't. That elbow sure helped." —***Bill Presley***, BRAKEMAN

"We had bad spots all through the Coquihalla. But we didn't go very fast down there, 15-18 miles an hour was top speed with a freight train. You didn't let it get away on you if you weren't going any faster than that. Coming up you were working uphill. It was treacherous country, but relatively safe. Once in a while a washout or a big rock would sneak up on you. From Penticton, westward to Brookmere, the worst part would be from Faulder up to Kirton in the Faulder Canyon we called it. The rest of it was pretty well clear to Brookmere; it wasn't bad at all." —***Dick Broccolo***, ENGINEER

"Coming home from Portland, the American highways were blocked and the only way we could get home to Penticton was to put our car on a flatcar. It turned out the Coquihalla was blocked. It took us 72 hours to get from Vancouver instead of 8 or 12." —***Herb McGregor***

Coquihalla Snowsheds

The Coquihalla required 15 snowsheds, built in 1915-1920, clustered between Romeo, Mile 24.1, and Iago, Mile 29.6.

Shed No.	Mileage	Length in feet* Early Years	1947
1	23.8	1000 or 960	—
2	24.0	186 (2-track)	—
3	24.1/.2	600 (2-track)	—
4	24.3	350	—
5	24.4	430	374
6	24.5	250	—
7	24.7	560 (1130 max.)	—
8	24.9	600	—
9	25.2	408	—
10	26.0	1080	—
11	26.3	1400	230
12	26.6	1412	420
13	26.8	144	—
14	26.9	280	290
15	28.2	360	322

By the 1930s nearly all sheds were due for replacement at a cost of over $1,000,000. Instead, the pass was closed for longer periods and all but critical sheds removed.

* Length varied over the years as a result of damage and repairs. Based on KVR/CPR documents but sources differ.

Snowsheds were the first line of defence against the snow and slides. Romeo (far left) has a light covering, but the photo at left shows the depths of snow that could sweep down. —DAVE WILKIE COLLECTION

"Out of the nine years I was in the running trade, I don't think it was open more than two or three times all winter. It hardly ever shut until January. The slide periods would start in January or February and then you'd start bucking it open in March." —***Alan Palm***, CONDUCTOR

"It really was Romeo to Portia that was the bad snow country. Just below Slide Creek, Mile 25, to Iago was the worst. Even with bulldozers and spreaders you didn't have the reliability you needed." —***Fred Joplin***, DIVISION ENGINEER

The Rotary Snowplows—"The 400802 was at Brookmere, and the 400805 was at Hope. When they discontinued the terminal at Hope, about 1926, they moved the 805 to Brookmere. We had two of them there until about 1931 or '32 when the 400802 was sent to the Kootenay Division. The 802 was the red rotary and the 805 was the black rotary. That's how they were identified. When I was in train service, the 805 was the one that was operating.

"I made several trips on rotary plows before I started braking. There was quite a bit of damage done to the wires and communications as a result of the rotary throwing snow right into the wires and breaking them, tangling them up. . . . So there was generally a line man or a climber with them to watch it.

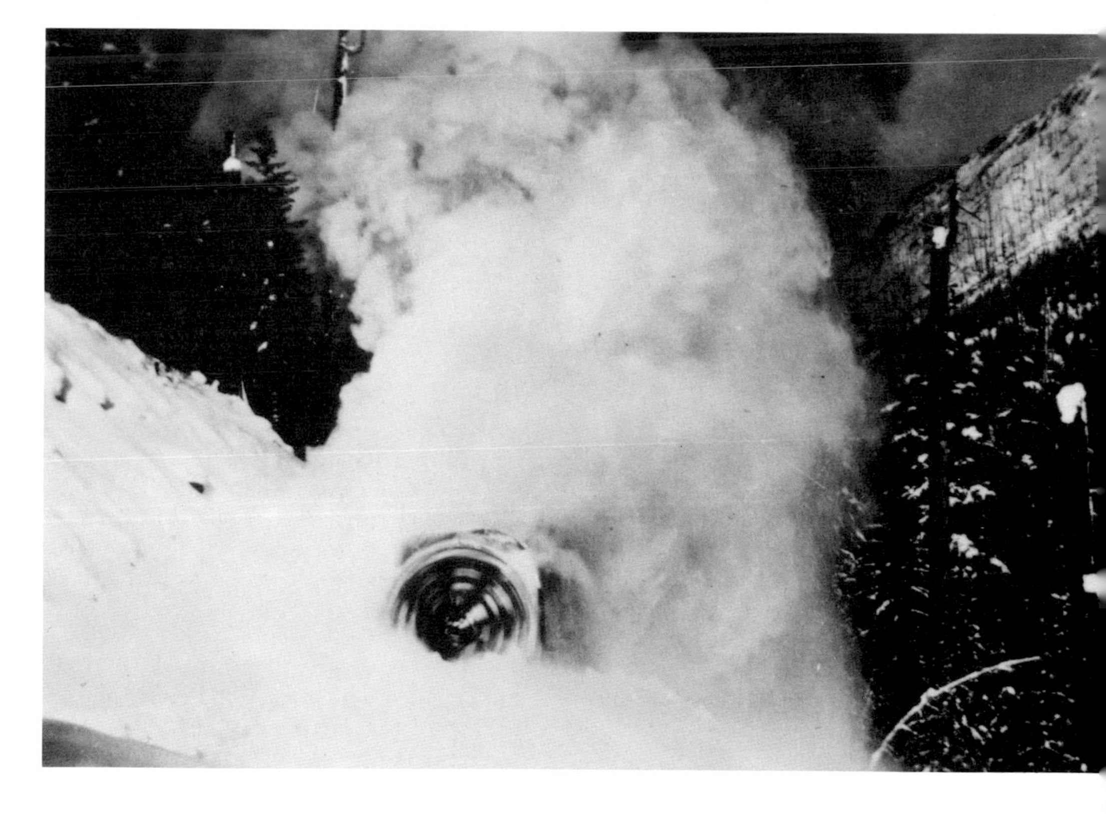

The rotary snowplow was a thundering apparition that was the best the railroaders had for fighting snow. Pushed by locomotives and powered by its own boiler, the rotary created a storm of its own. Ralph A. Welford photographed this Coquihalla scene in 1921. —PENTICTON MUSEUM, 37-2019

"I think this would be in about January '35, the winter of the big snow. We went east with the rotary and there were two engines. The second followed behind the first one. It was beautiful. There must have been four or five feet of new light snow and the rotary worked perfectly. We got down the Manning Flats, and there was a big pile of snow, and the rotary got stuck. The rotary and one engine. We were following with the second engine and caboose. When they got stuck, the second engine came up and coupled up and they were working back and forth, trying to free the thing. I was in the cab of the second engine and we got steam and exhaust coming back. You couldn't see a thing. As we started back, the whistle started to blow and the engineer, Charlie Craney, says, 'Well we're going to get her out of here now and we're not going to stop.' So he didn't stop. We backed up quite a distance and then stopped. We looked out and all we had was the tender of the rotary. The rest of it was still back in the slide. It broke apart between the rotary and tender. Not humorous, but surprising. The troubles we had.

"Joe Collett was firing on the rotary, and he said he damn near got it because he was on the deck between the rotary and the tender. It could have been quite dangerous."
—*Bill Presley*, BRAKEMAN

Rotary 400802 fought many battles in the Coquihalla before being transferred to Nelson. Built in 1888 to help keep the main line open, it is shown at Nelson on May 8, 1949. Bulldozers eventually proved to be more effective. —JIM HOPE

The rotaries could be very efficient, cutting through snow and blowing it clear. The photo shows how damage could be done to the telegraph lines. —BILL PRESLEY

Conditions were miserable and hours endless but the crews never held back. A. A. Smith, trainmaster, and the foreman of the Japanese labour gang stand beside the rotary. —DICK BROCCOLO COLLECTION

When they reached a snowshed, the rotary crews would have to back out, to make room for labourers to clear the entrance. —BILL PRESLEY

Closing the Coquihalla

The pass might be closed for just a few days, but it could be snowed-in for months, for example: December 14, 1917 to May 31, 1918; January 20, 1921 to May 22, 1921. In the 1930s, it was routinely closed for two to four months. Rock slides and damage to sheds closed the line for six months in 1938-1939. In the first 30 years only 1940-1941 saw no closings although in 1943-1944 just one day was lost.

Abandonment was considered in the 1920s but the subsidies and political considerations deferred action. In the early 1930s, abandonment was again reviewed and, ironically, the Great Northern's payments for running rights, and savings from not replacing snowsheds, justified retaining the line. Extra costs to operate via Spences Bridge were just $7,000 a month. By the time the Coquihalla agreement was ended and the CPR bought the GN trackage between Brookmere and Princeton, the Second World War was reaching a climax and then the post-War years were prosperous, postponing thoughts of abandonment until the full impact of highway construction hit in the 1950s.

During the Second World War, Japanese-Canadians interned at Tashme, east of Hope, were recruited to form a Bridge and Building gang to work in the Coquihalla. —PRIVATE COLLECTION

The plow train has nearly reached a snowshed after cutting through slides as high as the locomotive.
—DICK BROCCOLO COLLECTION

A Coquihalla plow train, at right, from the diesel years. A plow was run at each end of the locomotive so that the train could not be cut off by slides. This arrangement also meant that the train did not need to be turned. —ALBERT MARTINO

"Riding the plow, you'd give the one whistle just before you hit the slide. The engineer would put it into reverse so that you hit the slide with full force but you were starting to back up too. That way you didn't get stuck." —*Bill Quail*, BRAKEMAN

Plow service on the Coquihalla—"On a regular snowplow, you'd just have plow, engine, tender and caboose. The engine crew would have lunchboxes and the same with the plow crew. It was routine. You'd be called at Brookmere for the plow and you'd go down as far as Portia and turn on the wye and wait until you were just ahead of the passenger No. 12, coming up, and you'd come back up the hill ahead of 12.

"I can remember . . . between Romeo and Coquihalla in places where there had been slides, the snow embankment would be 10 and 12 feet high, even on the low side, like you were going down a real cut.

"When you were bucking slides with the wing plow, you'd hit a slide and back away sometimes, the whole face of the slide would be just the shape of the plow. You couldn't go in and hit it like that. You had to put men up on top of the slide and they'd shovel snow down to make a cushion; it would be like hitting a brick wall otherwise." —*Bill Presley*, BRAKEMAN

"One of the men working in Coquihalla [in the 1950s] was the famous track patrolman Wong Gee. He had enlisted in the Kettle Valley in 1922 and had been a track patrolman at Iago and Romeo, mostly Iago, his entire career. He worked as a section man occasionally, but essentially his job was patrolling track at night and he knew every inch—all the avalanche chutes and snowslides. One night I went out with him. The guy only weighed about 90 pounds. He said, 'We go for a walk.' Then later 'This is a good place, we walk slow, easy.' A little further on, 'This a bad place, we go like hell.' I hung onto his belt and we fled across the avalanche chute because you never knew when they'd come down." —ANON

In the chilling cold of a Coquihalla snowstorm, the men shovel snow down into the cut made by the plow to cushion the impact of the plow train's next run at the slide. —DICK BROCCOLO COLLECTION

"If it got to be daylight and a bit too warm, slides might start coming down. You'd go out on a bridge or another safe spot with the plow train. You wouldn't know what was coming down because the heat would loosen the top stuff. You'd go back and the line could be all plugged up again." —*Bill Quail*, BRAKEMAN

"We would go out every night with the plow. We were running two passenger trains [after the Second World War]. We would go to Portia, out of Brookmere, and we would get to about 1.5 miles west of Iago where we could see either 46 or 12 coming. We had a run ahead order, which meant we could run on their time. Once we saw the train just west of Portia, we'd scamper ahead of it and sit on the curve just east of Romeo. When the train came into Romeo, we'd go ahead of it to Coquihalla. When it went by, we'd go back down to Portia and wait and do the same thing for the next train. Then we'd go back to Brookmere.

"For the westbounds, we'd start out of Brookmere in the morning, just ahead of the passenger. We'd plow to Portia and wait while the passenger train went by. Then we'd do what we called the 'cleanup service.' That was with the spreader and he'd spend the rest of the day cleaning up. We would comb all the snow. We'd already daylighted the cuts so you could use the main arm of the spreader right the way through. The spreader would reach out 16 feet from the tracks. We did this day after day in the winter." —*Fred Joplin*, DIVISION ENGINEER

Bob Suzuki, remembered as a "true, tough, resourceful, Coquihalla warrior" by other Kettle Valley veterans, was section foreman at Romeo in the 1940s. He lived alone and during the winter kept full boxes of 40 percent Forcite dynamite under his bed to keep it warm and dry for use with the snowplow. —PRIVATE COLLECTION

"It was not uncommon for the Coquihalla assigned snowplow to make 15,000 snowplow miles in one winter. When you consider that from Coquihalla to Portia, is about 15 miles, to make 15,000 snowplow miles you've got to make a hell of a lot of trips up and down. It came mostly in December, January and February. When they weren't plowing, they would be spreading with a Jordan Spreader. The idea is to move the snow as far away from the track as possible.

"During the winter months, when the passenger train used to leave Brookmere around 6 or 7 o'clock in the evening, it usually took it two hours and a bit to get to Hope. We often didn't think of going to bed until we heard from the operator at Hope saying he's here. Many times, things were done that were absolutely illegal. For example, the snowplow would leave Portia to go back up to Coquihalla and if the conductor and the engineer on the passenger train following weren't too prissy about the rules, they'd be right on the plow's tail. The conductor on the snowplow would have a lighted red fusee on the caboose burning all the time. The train would follow by the light of that fusee. That's a total no in operating rules. You do that under the penalty of instant death. Technically, the plow is to go to the next siding or station and advise the dispatcher that it got there and then the passenger train can follow from the station behind and come up. The trouble is in the intervening half hour or more, all hell has broken loose. You come around the corner and you've got a wall of snow maybe 50 feet deep. —ANON

"The Coquihalla was a different thing. It wasn't a full-year operation because we had to close down sometimes for months in the wintertime. It was very expensive between the snowsheds and tunnels. Maintenance was terrible on it. The Great Northern Railway had the right to run over the CPR tracks. By the early 1940s they were anxious to relinquish their rights because under agreement they had to pay rental and part of the maintenance on the Coquihalla Subdivision. They still, for years, wanted to retain the right at some time to run to Vancouver. —*Jack Petley*, LATER ASSISTANT SUPERINTENDENT AT PENTICTON

Braking down the Coquihalla—"You'd get to Coquihalla and you'd put the retainers up and the engineer would make an eight- or nine-pound reduction. Every car is equipped with a retaining valve up by the brakewheel. You put that up and it retards the exhaust from the brake cylinder and that holds back the air and gives you sufficient time to repump and recharge your train line. Get it back up to 70 pounds. With them up, you'd wait a while till they released a bit but still retaining, then you'd get going. You'd stop at Iago for 15 or 20 minutes for a thermal test; that's to allow the heat to distribute through the wheels. Then you'd drop down and do the same thing at Jessica. A passenger train would only make one. They'd stop at Portia when they were going downhill. You'd leave the retainers up until a mile out of Hope, then knock the retainers down on the fly. You would just go over the top of the train and individually knock them down. Mostly just lean over and knock them down with your foot.

"One of the greatest things I think most people on the Kettle learned was a very deep respect for George Westinghouse, the inventor of the air brake; a real respect and appreciation of the air brake." —*Bill Presley*, BRAKEMAN

The Coquihalla could be spectacular. The fireman on the pusher is having troubles if the huge plume of black smoke is any indication. Conductor J. H. Pride shows how to use his brake club. —LANCE CAMP COLLECTION; DICK BROCCOLO COLLECTION

WRECKS AND MISHAPS

Kettle Valley railroaders often recall the accidents and wrecks that were a seemingly constant hazard in the mountain passes. Most men experienced some derailments or mishaps during their careers. For the majority, they were not serious but for a few they were fatal or left lasting injuries. But wrecks were not everyday happenings. Crews were well trained and highly conscious of the dangers of operating carelessly or with malfunctioning equipment. Trains ran through the passes, over the steep grades and in the worst winter weather with an amazing safety record year after year. Nevertheless, the terrain and the weather made some accidents a virtual certainty.

Examples of wrecks and minor accidents on the Kettle Valley include the following: engines 583 and 566 collided headon north of Brookmere when 583 failed to register at Brodie with no serious injuries to the engine crews; locomotive 3688 fell through a bridge over the Tulameen River at Mile 77.5, west of Princeton, in December 1937 and W. E. "Pony" Moore, brakeman, was killed; engine 5178 on Train No. 11 hit rocks west of Romeo in November 1941 killing Engineer Harry O. B. "Oil Burner" McDonald and Fireman Pete Riley; engine 907 blew up in the Brookmere roundhouse killing watchmen Rasmussen; the engines of No. 11 and No. 12 sideswiped each other at Jellicoe on October 14, 1950 in a spectacular wreck that nearly destroyed the section house; and in a well photographed incident Train No. 12 derailed on a washout within sight of Penticton on November 29, 1949.

Rocks on the Tracks . . .
Mileage 88.6 on the Princeton Sub
. . . March 29, 1948

"We were running ahead of Train No. 45 and I was firing for Joe Collett, on the 5213, a stoker engine. I had the engine just poppin' away hot and he was just working the hell out of it. Then I heard Joe holler, he plugged her and the next thing, we were over on our side, bouncing. I had Joe, the rakes, brakeman Jim McQuire, all the oil cans and everything on top of me. Then we came to a shaking halt. The whistle stuck, blowing to beat heck. . . . Nobody was hurt. All the cars telescoped behind." —*Dick Broccolo*, ENGINEER

The boiler explosion of Tenwheeler 907 at Brookmere on March 21, 1949, wrecked the enginehouse and killed the locomotive watchman. —DICK BROCCOLO COLLECTION

The Worst Wreck, September 5, 1926—"A freight crew was marshalled in Brookmere yard. . . . The road engine was the 3401; Engineer Bob Marks and Fireman Ray Letts. The helper engine had Engineer Bill Osborne and Fireman Bob Barwick. It was on the rear of the train, just ahead of the caboose. Engineer Smokey Bill Clapperton, who was living at Hope, was working at Brookmere and he was deadheading from Brookmere to Hope. . . .

"The train proceeded from Brookmere and after leaving the summit at Coquihalla. Smokey, who was in the cupola of the caboose and could watch the air gauge there could see that Engineer Marks was having troubles to control the speed of the train. It became apparent to him that the train was then out of speed control so he got over to the cab of the helper engine and advised them that the engineer on the head end was in trouble and they should try and close the angle cocks on the front end of their engine and cut off from the train as they were only a detriment to the rest of the train. Fireman Barwick was able to close the angle cock and break the hose and pull the pin. They followed the train down the mountain.

"The conductor, Jack Quinn, and brakemen Mickey Stringer and Ollie Johnston, were on top of the train, setting handbrakes to try and gain control of the speed of the train. . . . About a half mile further on, the head engine left the track on a bridge [just past Jessica] and the engine and train went into the canyon. Because of the excessive heat from the brakes, the oily waste in the journals of the cars caught fire and the whole train burned up. Engineer Marks, Conductor

Jack Quinn and brakemen Ollie Johnson and Mick Stringer were all killed as well a number of transients riding on top of the train. The exact number was not known. . . . The train crew and Engineer Marks were all friends of mine, fellow workers. . . .

"The cause of the wreck has been attributed to failure of manpower, but . . . in many minds, the full cause of the wreck will never be known."
—*F. Perley McPherson*, CONDUCTOR IN A REMINISCENCE HE TAPED MANY YEARS LATER

"Bob, they said, there weren't any tires left on his engine. They'd all come off. He'd been sanding and using his engine brakes, the tires just got red hot and came off."
—*Gordon Fulkerson*, ENGINEER

"The whole thing went over the side at Jessica. Ray Letts bailed out [other accounts report that he was thrown from the train while helping with the brakes] into a pile of cinders and survived. But he would never give a statement. Until he died, he had the nickname 'Clammy,' Clammy Letts." —ANON

The wreck of the 3231 recalled on the next page. —GORDON FULKERSON COLLECTION

The aftermath of the wreck that cost Jack Crosby his life. The tender jackknifed, the baggage car was flung perpendicular to the tracks and the following coach crushed into the cab.
—DICK BROCCOLO COLLECTION

Crosby's Wreck

"It was the first time I ever heard my dad use harsh language. The passenger cars were scattered all over the place. They heard the train coming in Beaverdell and then it was all silent. Then a while later they saw a fellow coming up the track. They got a speeder and headed down the track to help out. Engineer Crosby was killed. Crosby's widow married Bob Marks who piled up at Jessica in 1926 and was killed." —*Glen Morley*, RECALLING THE WRECK OF TRAIN NO. 11 SOUTH OF BEAVERDELL ON NOVEMBER 11, 1924

"Kidney Foot" and the 3231

"After 1915, 1916, they sent us a bunch of 3200s. They were just a little smaller than 34s [that came later]. They were a deckless engine. Just had a steel plank, the apron [between the back of the boiler and the tender]. They were dangerous things.

"I was firing for Sid Cornock on the east side. They had the old 3231. It was the 24th of May, 1921. Sid laid off and Oscar Cummings took his trip. . . . Just about a mile west of Taurus, I heard Oscar shout, 'Plug Her!' I jumped for the cab from the apron, because there was no sense of being down in between there. Just as I jumped, she hit the rockslide. It wasn't a big one, but there was one great big rock in it and it turned the engine over on Oscar's side. I was scared . . . the injector broke and steam was blowing everywhere. I hadn't been firing very long. So I climb over the rocks and run up the tracks until things cleared. The steam blew off and cleared up, I came back and Oscar and the train crew are looking around, figuring that I was in the wreck. They couldn't find me anywhere. So Oscar said, 'Here comes that kidney-footed son of a bitch. We couldn't kill him.' It stuck like that. I was known as that right till I quit."

—***Gordon Fulkerson***, ENGINEER

The abutment on the Kettle River bridge near Rock Creek washed out in April 1918, leaving a routine but difficult task for the Bridge & Building gang.
—PENTICTON MUSEUM, 37-2019

On October 14, 1950, the 5221 and 5121 were ordered to "meet" at Jellicoe but instead they collided.
—LANCE CAMP COLLECTION

THE KETTLE VALLEY EXPRESS & THE KOOTENAY EXPRESS

Passenger service across the southern Interior was synonymous with two trains, the westbound *Kootenay Express*, Train No. 11, and the eastbound *Kettle Valley Express*, No. 12 introduced after the end of the First World War. During the war years, passenger services varied but were often limited to just three passenger trains a week each way over the Kettle Valley. The No. 11 and No. 12 wound their way at a leisurely pace between Medicine Hat,* Alberta, and Vancouver, B.C., a distance of 962 miles (1548 km). They connected dozens of communities ranging in size from the cities of Cranbrook, Nelson and Penticton to tiny or now-forgotten places such as Carmi or Jellicoe. The trains carried mail, express, merchandise and passengers and were many people's most important link with the rest of the world.

"It is as if the traveller were a passenger in an aeroplane; the train which is curving back and forth seems to be drifting on the wind. . . . Such is the sensation of being carried at a rapid pace to touch dizzying heights! But the passenger should settle back in his chair and decline to become panicky. Greater thrills are in store. This is but a practice exhibition for the feats that the train is to perform later in the day.

"It will be many years . . . before it fails to thrill even the most seasoned tourist who is used to trestles, bridges, mountains and lakes." —***Archie Bell***, *British Columbia and Beyond*, 1918

"The Kettle Valley Railway itself originally started at Midway, and the part through to Alberta was made up of the Columbia & Western and the Canadian Pacific, but everybody used to talk about the Kettle Valley Line as the whole thing that the train ran on. The *Kettle Valley Express*—people knew the name of it." —***Tom Barnes***, DINING CAR COOK

"No. 11 would come in from Nelson and then head into the Penticton station on the waterfront, right through town. To go back out he would back out to South Penticton and layover for 20 minutes for servicing. No. 12 arriving from the west came in and backed into downtown. . . . On Saturday mornings, several of us kids would pile onto the observation car and ride as it backed up to South Penticton. They would turn a blind eye to us unless they were very busy." —***Glen Morley***

The *Kootenay Express* is dwarfed by the steel bridge over the West Fork of Canyon Creek in Myra Canyon. Taken soon after the replacement of the wooden trestle with a steel structure in 1932, the photo shows a typical four-car train headed by the 588, a D9 Tenwheeler. The train includes a baggage and mail car, a coach, sleeper and a beautiful open-platform, cafe-parlour-observation car. Steel passenger cars began to replace the aging wooden cars at this time but the cafe-parlour is still of wooden construction. —PENTICTON MUSEUM

"I worked at Beaverdell at the Highland Lass Mine in the winter of 1933-1934. Sometimes, we had a long weekend or at Christmas. . . . We'd pick up the train at Beaverdell and come on down to Kelowna. We got off at McCulloch, and the train carried on to Penticton. Many people that were coming to Kelowna would carry on by train to Penticton, pick up the *Sicamous* or the *Okanagan*, and come back to Kelowna. Most of us fellows would take the shortcut, and come down by the stage—a big old Hudson Sedan. It was a gamble for him, because sometimes there wouldn't be anybody getting off the train and he'd come back empty; other times, he'd be plugged. When we came down, the snow was very deep and we had an awful time. We'd have to take turns shovelling snow to get down. Normally it took about an hour and a half coming down, it was slow going." —***Bill Knowles***

"I was aware that people were nervous. You could feel the tension as you started down. The Coquihalla River is right beside you and it suddenly just drops away as you leave from the summit. They would be very careful going down there. Down by the Quintette Tunnels, there is a curve going into them. You could feel a sigh of relief as you got down into the last stretch." —***Glen Morley***

* Passengers would change trains at Dunmore, Alberta a short distance east of Medicine Hat.

The *Kettle Valley Express* rounds Ladner Creek bridge as it climbs towards Coquihalla Summit in a photo from about 1951. Unlike many other structures in the Coquihalla, it survived the dismantling of the railway and later highway construction. —NICHOLAS MORANT

Taking the Train to School—Athena Apostoli had to travel from her home at Tulameen to Princeton to complete her last two years of high school.

"The train came through about 2:30, 3:00 in the morning. There was no mail on Mondays. It stopped for mail and newspapers, every day but Monday mornings. I'd go home weekends and be going back to school Monday mornings, so I'd have to use my flashlight, and flash or flag the train down. They were waiting for me. I'd get on the train and ride about three quarters of an hour to Princeton.

"There was some of the most beautiful scenery I ever saw in the wintertime. Moonlight night, riding that train, and the river right beside you and the snow and the ice. You could see a bit of the river, but most of it would be frozen over. Just beautiful. . . . Moonlight nights there were just fantastic. Then I'd get into Princeton and the lady I stayed with would have hot bricks in my bed to keep my feet warm in the wintertime. The trainmen got so that they'd know me." *—Athena Apostoli*

"I enjoyed trips to Vancouver. I just loved looking down and seeing the river way down below [in the Coquihalla]. My mother didn't want to look. I'd say, 'Mum, come and look at the beautiful scenery.' 'Never mind,' she says.

"I remember the trestles with all the woodwork. Enormous. I found it quite thrilling. I wasn't at all afraid. We'd just go coach. There was always a man serving sandwiches, candy and coffee. We would very seldom take a lunch. The men who worked on the train were very good. They knew exactly when you were getting off and they'd let you know ahead of time." *—Athena Apostoli*

"Your conduct and intercourse with passengers is governed by the most scrupulous regard for courtesy, kindness and gentlemanly bearing, answering (if possible) all questions. . . ." —CANADIAN PACIFIC RAILWAY, PRIVATE INSTRUCTIONS TO TRAIN CONDUCTORS, NO. 9

"Lightning Jesus, lady, you need binoculars!" —***Bill Percival***, 'PAYROLL BILL,' CONDUCTOR, SPEAKING TO A WOMAN TRAVELLER UNABLE TO SEE A MOUNTAIN GOAT FROM THE TRAIN. QUOTED IN *Railroad Magazine*, AUGUST 1950

"Passenger trains must not exceed a speed of one mile in two minutes (30 miles per hour) and freight trains must not exceed a speed of one mile in four minutes (15 miles per hour) when descending grade Chute Lake to South Penticton.

Trains must not exceed a speed of one mile in four minutes between mileage 83.6 and 88 [Myra and two miles east of Ruth].

All Westbound trains will stop at least ten minutes at Glenfir and make thermal test in accordance with rule 27c of the rules for the operation and inspection of air brakes. If any wheels are excessively heated they must be allowed time to cool and then be closely watched until the foot of the grade is reached.

"All Westbound passenger trains will stop at Glenfir and if any wheels are excessively heated they must be allowed time to cool." —INSTRUCTIONS, CARMI SUBDIVISION, KETTLE VALLEY RAILWAY, EMPLOYEES' TIMETABLE, NO. 27, MAY 15, 1927

"Faye Carruthers and the Collins brothers were some of the black porters. They all lived in Vancouver and worked on the passenger trains, the 11 and 12 and the senior ones often took the 45 and 46 to Penticton. They had been on them for years and knew more about them than we ever did, I think. They were fine people. At that time, only Caucasions could belong to the union."
—*Bill Quail*, BRAKEMAN

Capturing a breathtaking view, Gib Kennedy photographed Canyon Creek's West Fork bridge at mile 87.9 in Myra Canyon in August 1950. The sleeping cars are the *Newcastle* and the *Naples*.
—W. GIBSON KENNEDY

Dining in the cafe-parlour cars on the Kettle Valley passenger trains was a treat long remembered by travellers. The cars featured an 18-seat dining area with all of the refinements of service on the main line except for a somewhat more restricted menu. Sparkling white linen tablecloths and napkins, gleaming silver service and CPR-monogrammed china were all part of the service. The wide-based water pitchers were part of each table setting.

On this trip, about 1949, Betty Kennedy enjoys a meal on Train No. 11 between Fife and Cascade. At this point, the train is still east of the Kettle Valley, but the cafe-parlour car will be part of the train until it reaches Penticton.
—W. GIBSON KENNEDY

"West Summerland—West Summerland next stop."
—CONDUCTOR'S ANNOUNCEMENT

Bacon and Eggs, Prime Rib and Open-Platform Parlour Cars

"There'd be fresh fruit and stuff brought on [at Penticton] and it would always be a feature. The CPR always used to serve the feature of the area. . . . Two of us were in the kitchen and two of us would be waiting on the tables. If it was light, there would only be one man working on the tables. I know that one waiter had a tough time if there were 12 seats keeping up with the service. It was a very restricted menu on a cafe car. Perhaps half the amount on a full diner. The most popular thing was bacon and eggs. It was always great on the CPR." —*Tom Barnes*, DINING CAR COOK

"They were wonderful meals—CPR meals—with silverware and white linen tablecloths and napkins." —*Glen Morley*

"I was leaving Vancouver on No. 12 [about 1954] and on the tail end that day it was either the observation car *Fort Steele* or *Fort Simpson*. . . . I was in the sleeping car ahead of it. Just after we left Vancouver, I asked the conductor if it would be all right if I went back and rode on the observation platform. I thought this was probably my last ride on an open-end observation car. So I opened the door, and dragged one of the big chesterfield chairs through and got it out onto the platform and I sat there and had my feet up on the railing. I was just in my glory! When we went through Mission station people were there and I waved at them. They looked up kind of startled at this guy sitting on the back. I stayed out there till we were past Hope and by now it's getting dark, about 11:00. We started heading up into the Coquihalla and it started to pour rain so . . . I went back to the sleeper and went to bed." —*L. S. Morrison*

CANADIAN PACIFIC DINING CAR SERVICE

KOOTENAY EXPRESS

BREAKFAST

A LA CARTE

FRUITS, ETC.

BAKED PEAR 15, WITH CREAM 25
BAKED APPLE 15, WITH CREAM 25 GRAPEFRUIT (HALF) 30
PEACHES IN SYRUP 25 APPLE SAUCE 25
PRUNES WITH CREAM 30 BANANAS WITH CREAM 25
TOMATO JUICE COCKTAIL 25 GRAPE JUICE 20 ORANGE JUICE 35
ASSORTED FRESH FRUIT 35

CEREALS WITH MILK 20, WITH CREAM 30

FISH

BROILED OR FRIED SALMON, CODFISH OR SOLE 70
FISH CAKES 40, WITH BACON 50
KIPPERED HERRING, SWEET POTATO 70

CHOPS, STEAKS, ETC.—FROM THE GRILL

BROILED OR FRIED SPRING CHICKEN, HALF 1.25 (20 MINUTES)
"RED BRAND" SIRLOIN STEAK 1.50 "RED BRAND" SMALL STEAK 1.00
BROILED OR FRIED HAM (FULL CUT) 65 LAMB CHOPS (ONE) 45 (TWO) 85
HAM ½ CUT WITH 1 EGG 55, WITH 2 EGGS 65 BACON (3 STRIPS) 35 (6 STRIPS) 65
BACON AND EGGS 65
CALF'S LIVER WITH BACON 75
(Strip of Bacon served with other Orders 15, or Individual Mushrooms 25)

EGGS, OMELETS, ETC.

BOILED (ONE) 20 (TWO) 35 SCRAMBLED 35 FRIED (ONE) 20 (TWO) 35
POACHED ON TOAST (ONE) 20 (TWO) 40
PLAIN 45 TOMATO OR CHEESE 50 JELLY, HAM OR SPANISH 60
CHICKEN OMELET 60 OMELET WITH RED CHERRIES 60
FRENCH TOAST WITH JELLY 30

FRENCH FRIED OR HASHED BROWNED POTATOES 25
LYONNAISE POTATOES 25

IT is with pleasure and pride that we call attention to the desire and willingness of all our employees to give their utmost in service and special attention and they as well as ourselves would appreciate your criticisms as well as your commendations.

KOOTENAY EXPRESS

BREAKFAST

A LA CARTE
Continued

MARMALADE, JAMS OR JELLIES 15
(IN INDIVIDUAL JARS)

QUINCE JELLY BRAMBLEBERRY JELLY CRABAPPLE JELLY
STRAWBERRY JAM RASPBERRY JAM
ORANGE OR GRAPEFRUIT MARMALADE

PRESERVED FRUITS 25
(IN INDIVIDUAL JARS)

PINEAPPLE RASPBERRIES RED CHERRIES STRAWBERRIES
PRESERVED RED CHERRIES WITH HOT BISCUITS 35
PRESERVED FIGS 40
INDIVIDUAL CANADIAN COMB OR STRAINED HONEY 25

BREAD AND BUTTER SERVICE PER PERSON

BRAN OR CORN MUFFINS 15
TOAST 15 HOT ROLLS, BROWN OR WHITE 15
MILK TOAST 30 CREAM TOAST 40
WHITE, BROWN AND RAISIN BREAD 15 RY-KRISP HEALTH BREAD 15
GRIDDLE CAKES, MAPLE SYRUP 35

TEA, COFFEE, ETC.

COFFEE, POT, 25, SERVED WITH HOT MILK OR CREAM TEA, POT 25
KAFFEE HAG 25 INSTANT POSTUM 25 COCOA, POT 25
INDIVIDUAL SEALED BOTTLE MILK 15 BUTTERMILK 15
MALTED MILK 20 OVALTINE 20 NESTLE'S FOOD MILK 25
BOVRIL 25 HOT OXO 25
FLEISCHMANN'S YEAST, PER CAKE 10

PASSENGERS WILL KINDLY REFRAIN FROM SMOKING IN THIS ROOM.

WHEREVER you travel on the Canadian Pacific, you will find the same desire to maintain that excellence of service for which the Company has been noted for over forty years. The seemingly effortless perfection of Canadian Pacific service is simply an infinite capacity for taking pains.

IT will be a great aid to the service and will avoid any possibility of mistakes if passengers will kindly ask for meal order blanks, and upon them will write their orders, because stewards and waiters are not allowed to serve any food without a meal check.

W. A. COOPER, Manager, Sleeping, Dining, Parlor Cars,
Station Restaurants and News Service, Montreal.

11-12 1-2 B. V-23

Excerpts from a 1923 *Kootenay Express* menu. —LANCE CAMP COLLECTION

Canadian Pacific
DINING CAR SERVICE

"Please write on meal check each item desired.

"Employees are not permitted to accept or serve orders given verbally." —1953 MENU

"Going down into Penticton from Chute Lake, getting there late at night, everybody would be up looking out the windows. The next morning you had to get up damned early because people would get on in Penticton and they would want to have breakfast. You were climbing up the hill, and they loved to sit in that little car and look out. It was beautiful. We really didn't have any kind of layover. It was in there at 11:30 or midnight and out at 4:00 or 5:00 in the morning. Sometimes we'd sleep in the parlour car and other times we'd get out and sleep in the bunkhouse. It was a tough job." —*Tom Barnes*, DINING CAR COOK

"In the little buffet-parlour, one of the meals I had was prime rib with hash browns; it was really good. It was served in its own special silver platter, in its own juice. I was travelling on a pass and was in the day coach. After I finished my meal, I sat in the little lounge in the end of the car and the car attendant came and said, 'I'm sorry, sir, but you'll have to go back up to the day coach because you're not a first-class passenger.'" —*L. S. Morrison*

Diversions of traffic from the main line began as early as the summer of 1916. Even a silk train was rerouted but it was wrecked at Merritt when it hit an engine switching in the yards. The most important diversion of main line traffic was in 1929 after the collapse of part of Surprise Creek Bridge in the Selkirk Mountains. The Kettle Valley—Kootenay route became the only available Canadian Pacific line across British Columbia. This experience, and a decision to allow longer closings of the Coquihalla, prompted further upgrading of bridges and other improvements which permitted larger locomotives to be used on the Kettle Valley. Floods, washouts or storms caused diversions from the main line and the almost annual closures of the Coquihalla forced Kettle Valley traffic to the main line via Spences Bridge to Vancouver.

After the Surprise Creek Bridge Collapsed—"They diverted all freight over the Kettle Valley. Lots of times we'd have a train out of here every 20 minutes. They shipped in a whole lot more 3200s. . . . They couldn't take a bigger engine than that over to Midway because there were bridges . . . that wouldn't take a larger engine. Most of them had been to the backshop to be overhauled. You'd get one of them, and compared to one of our engines, they really steamed.

"They had men from all over the place—boomers and everything else—some from way down in the States and men from the prairies, and from the main line, Revelstoke and Kamloops, Cranbrook and places like that. There was lots of times there would only be one man you'd know. Maybe it'd be the engineer or your conductor. You wouldn't know the other guys, they'd be strangers. Boy, we made good miles then, I tell you. I remember going east with Burt McLellan one trip, we had a 3200. When we got over to Rock Creek, they told us we'd have to wait there an hour or so, so the Grand Forks short crews [who worked between Grand Forks and Midway] could do the switching and get out of Midway because there wasn't room. So they held us there at Rock Creek for about an hour. Then we went into Midway and waited on the main line for damn near another hour. I think we were on that engine 22 hours. There were some long trips then, I tell you." —***Burt Lye***, ENGINEER

Coquhilla Diversions—There were also many times when the Coquihalla was closed and Kettle Valley traffic was diverted north, "around the Horn," via Spences Bridge. The reference, Gib Kennedy recalled, was to how vessels would have to take the long route around Cape Horn when the Panama Canal was closed periodically from landslides.

"In the fall of 1949, we had a lot of floods and that damaged the Coquihalla. We hadn't really recovered from the '48 flood damage during the summer of '49. In the fall of '49 we got slides and floods and everything else so we closed the Coquihalla down. We ran everything through the Merritt Sub. That winter was terrible in the Fraser Canyon. Once the weather had knocked out the Coquihalla, it decided to knock out the main line.

"If you get a warm front in November, November rains, after snow in October; that's something you've got to look out for. Same thing in February; you'd get a big melt and slides.

DETOURS

The First Detours over the Kettle Valley

"Main line C.P.R. trains are now running through Penticton on the Kettle Valley line. Washouts and slides on the C.P.R. near Golden and at other points have tied up C.P.R. transcontinental traffic . . . the parent line has been forced to come to the Kettle Valley for assistance.

"All transcontinental trains arriving during daylight hours are pulled down to the wharf to give the through passengers a glimpse of the town, the Incola Hotel and station and also the lake beach."
—*The Penticton Herald*, JUNE 29, 1916

An early diversion of mainline traffic over the Kettle Valley led to this embarrassing mishap. A silk train, powered by engine No. 522, collided with the tender of engine 3100 at Merritt on June 22, 1916. Fortunately no one was seriously injured including Conductor Gates who, as *The Nicola Valley News* reported, "was shot through a caboose window by the impact, without sustaining other than slight bruises and shock." —BILL PRESLEY COLLECTION

Bulldozers replaced the rotary snowplows and helped eliminate the need for many snowsheds in the Coquihalla by the 1940s but still the railway was frequently closed and detours were part of Kettle Valley operations until the Coquihalla was abandoned. Running the bulldozers required skill and stamina as this photo from the Coquihalla attests. D6 Caterpillars could be driven on the rails and with care, the operators could run them across bridges and trestles. By the time of abandonment only five snowsheds, all rebuilt, remained including No. 15 of which 172 feet (52.4 m) was of concrete.
—PENTICTON MUSEUM

"We detoured all that winter and that threw a hell of a load on the main line. We actually brought Kettle Valley snow crews down to help on the main line. Ernie Burlon, who was roadmaster at Brookmere, and Jack McKnight, the snowplow foreman, came down to the main line." —*Fred Joplin*, DIVISION ENGINEER

"It was when the Coquihalla was closed. That used to happen with somewhat monotonous regularity. I was on the passenger mainly. We usually had 5200s or 5100s. At that time, they were all oil-burning. I was there a couple of times. I was down there for a couple of weeks anyway [in 1948 or 1949]. The way the thing worked was, because of the two divisions being involved, the Vancouver Division and the Kettle Valley Division, they had to divide the mileage up between the crews. If there was one passenger train, like 11 and 12, that's considered one train, they'd have one Kettle Valley crew and one Kamloops crew to work the detour between North Bend and Brookmere. When 45 and 46 went on . . . then they'd have two Kettle Valley and two Kamloops crews and work the trains as they came. The regular crews brought them out of Vancouver, just the same as if they were going to Brookmere. North Bend was their destination terminal.

"The detours were all forced jobs, nobody bid on them. You would get called off the spare board to go down and relieve on them and then everybody on the spare board would be busy dodging . . . so they wouldn't have to go. There was a long layover in Brookmere and in North Bend. Even though North Bend is a nice little place, it wasn't all that attractive to lay over in.
—*Ernie Ottewell*, ENGINEER, RECALLING WORKING ON THE VANCOUVER DIVISION

Detours brought a variety of mainline locomotives to Brookmere but from there Kettle Valley engines and crews handled the traffic. The 5269 was at Brookmere during detours in the late 1940s.
—ERNIE OTTEWELL

The Kettle Valley received some of its finest power during the Depression years when the 5100s, handsome 2-8-2s, were assigned to the passenger runs and were based at Penticton and Nelson. After the Second World War, more 2-8-2s operated on the Kettle Valley, many of them rebuilt from 3600 and 3700 series 2-8-0s. High-drivered 4-6-2 Pacifics of the CPR's 2700 series, also made brief appearances as dieselization loomed in the early 1950s.

Gib Kennedy was in Nelson when the P1s entered service in 1933—"They were beautiful locomotives. . . . The train had just come in with the 5146 at the headend. Gold leaf on the tender lettering and gold leaf figures on the cab, white stripe on the running boards, white tires and the motion—the main driving rods and everything—was always gone over first thing in the morning at the shop with a burnisher before it was sent out to the train. You could see the burnishing marks on the valve motion. . . . They cleaned up those engines; they shone in fresh paint. They were sure smart-looking engines. The passenger train was the showcase for the Canadian Pacific. It had to look good and it did." —*W. Gibson Kennedy*

"I made my first trip running west with Perley McPherson, with a 5100. You could beat them fairly hard and they would take it. They were a good all-around engine. They weren't nearly as slippery as say some of those 5200s. A 5200, they'd see a rain shower 10 miles away and they'd start slippin'." —*Burt Lye*, ENGINEER

"Oil firing? Well, that was the ultimate. You didn't have to shovel coal. The stokers were nice, but I preferred oil-burners."
—*Ernie Ottewell*, VANCOUVER DIVISION ENGINEER ON KETTLE VALLEY DETOURS

"I just made the odd trip firing on oil-burners and an odd trip on [engines with] automatic stokers. When I started running they were automatic stokers and oil-burners and the fireman would sit over there with his feet crossed and look over at me laughing like hell! All he had to do was turn the valve. Oh gee!" —*Burt Lye*, ENGINEER

"[With oil-burners] it was like you were on holiday all the time. The job started getting very monotonous after that. You were too busy with the hand-fired and stoker engines and less busy with oil-burners. They were relatively simple to fire. . . ." —*Dick Broccolo*, ENGINEER

"I used to assist No. 11 from here [Penticton] over to Kirton nearly every night and then in the morning I'd be called to assist No. 12 to Chute Lake. With the 5121, I could make up 10 minutes every trip, but I couldn't with any other engine. I made my second trip [as engineer] on 5126, I went east. It was a real good engine too." —*Burt Lye*, ENGINEER

"We used to like the 5200s. They didn't last long, because the diesels were coming in. I don't think they lasted more than 10 years before they started scrapping them."
—*Gordon Fulkerson*, ENGINEER

Ready for winter with a snowplow big enough to handle substantial drifts of snow, the 5100, on Train No. 11, paused at Farron in 1943. The 5100s became inseparable from the Kettle Valley in its last two decades of steam operations.
—W. GIBSON KENNEDY

"New engines sure affected the trainmen and the enginemen. A fireman would step up from being an engine watchman to a fireman, and bigger power would come and back he'd be. Knocked back to a watchman again. For several years it was a pretty rough go for them. They'd be able to handle more tonnage but they'd be running fewer trains. The enginemen would get an increase in pay with heavier engines but it made no difference for the trainmen. The enginemen were paid by weight on drivers."
—*Bill Presley*, BRAKEMAN

Fireman's view of the tracks ahead from the 5100 on the Kootenay Division's Farron hill in November 1943. The constantly curving Kettle Valley and Kootenay divisions meant that the engineer and fireman had to be watching for any slides, washouts or other hazards.
—W. GIBSON KENNEDY

The 5100s were impressive locomotives from any angle. At left, the 5100 at Penticton on April 7, 1943, and below, the 5101 with Train No. 12 at the then new Penticton station. Both engines were coal-fired. At right, the 5101 on an eastbound extra at Carmi. The engine has a new cab, installed after a boiler explosion on a passenger train on November 25, 1944. These engines were built in 1912-1913 as the 5000 series P1a and P1b classes. They were modernized and were later fitted with feedwater heaters which contributed to their distinctive appearance. —JIM HOPE; ERNIE PLANT, FLOYD YATES COLLECTION; W. GIBSON KENNEDY

5101

The 3600s worked on the Kettle Valley until diesels took over. The 3665, an oil-burner from the Coast with a wartime headlight visor, was at Penticton on April 7, 1943. During the 1940s, more 3700s, like 3706 at Princeton on a Copper Mountain train, were assigned to the Kettle Valley. Pacifics, including 2707, once mainline passenger engines, worked as far as Penticton in the last years of steam operations. A few D9s, like the 572 at Penticton, survived until the late 1940s.
—JIM HOPE; W. GIBSON KENNEDY;
RAY MATTHEWS;
W. C. WHITTAKER COLLECTION

The 5200 2-8-2s were rebuilt from 3600 and 3700 class 2-8-0s in the late 1940s and were the most modern steam locomotives assigned to the Kettle Valley. The Kettle Valley and Kootenay Division P1n 5200s were later converted to oil-burners. The 5221 was photographed at Penticton. Heavy power for the pushers out of Penticton came in the 1940s with the assignment of one or two 5700 series 2-10-0s. These engines normally worked west to Kirton and east to Chute Lake. The 5788 is shown being turned at Penticton on August 9, 1953. —BOTH RAY MATTHEWS

Last Years of Steam

Helpers were a part of Kettle Valley steam operations until the diesels took over. An aged, although still well maintained, 3601 assists the 5211 on this wintry day at Penticton. —LANCE CAMP COLLECTION

At left, the 5259 leads No. 12, the *Kettle Valley Express*, through Carmi in the summer of 1950. —W. GIBSON KENNEDY

Drifting down into Penticton, the 5264, above and at right, leads a short freight through the orchards near Arawana on August 9, 1953. The brakeman, after having knocked down the retainers, relaxes on the top of the second boxcar. —BOTH RAY MATTHEWS

PART 3 *The Diesel Years*

When the Diesels Came

"I remember going down with all the rest of them with sleighs because there was still snow that spring. 'Oh look at these beautiful big units!' They were those great big streamlined ones at that time. We looked at them inside and out and thought they were wonderful. That was the deathknell for Brookmere. Whoever thought that this was going to happen? That's the kind Harry trained on and the older fellows didn't find it that difficult."
—*Til Percival*

Diesels came to the Kettle Valley Division and by the summer of 1954 steam power was just a memory. The new locomotives brought many changes but they could not change the weather. —ALLEN MANUEL, PENTICTON MUSEUM

The Canadian Locomotive Company sent two demonstrator diesels to run on the Kettle Valley in September 1951.
—BILL QUAIL

The diesel-electric revolution that swept North American railways in the late 1940s and 1950s came to the Canadian Pacific's southern British Columbia lines with an irresistible momentum. There were several reasons why the CPR made the Kettle Valley and Kootenay divisions the focus for dieselization. This program included all the trackage across southern British Columbia from Ruby Creek west of Hope all the way east to Crowsnest on the British Columbia-Alberta border. The mountainous nature of the route across southern British Columbia made the two divisions prime candidates because of the high fuel, maintenance and crew costs of running steam locomotives. Diesels could substantially reduce these expenses.

The extended range of diesels over steam locomotives and the ability to run several diesel units together in "multiple" with one engine crew meant that fewer stops were required for servicing and that helper engines could be eliminated. If diesels were dispatched with trains limited to the tonnage they could pull over the most restrictive grades then helpers were not needed. The cheaper operating costs of diesels in multiple unit configurations made it feasible to run the engines over parts of the line with less tonnage than they could handle. This gave them the capacity needed over the steepest grades. This type of operation was impractical with steam power. The plan worked and helpers disappeared across the Kettle Valley and Kootenay divisions although occasionally diesel helpers were used and for a brief period there were placed on heavy trains out of Penticton. Diesels were also able to complete trips over the line faster than steam power and a reduction was anticipated in running time of 24 hours for a freight train moving between Nelson and Ruby Creek. This cutting of transit time from 60 hours down to 36 hours also brought improvements in service for customers, saved on freight car charges and meant that fewer cars were needed to move the same tonnage because they could be turned around faster. Adding to the incentive to dieselize was a steady growth in traffic. Between 1939 and 1949, total cars handled over the Kettle Valley had increased from over 81,000 to 151,500 while earnings tripled.

Orders were placed with the three major Canadian diesel builders: the Canadian Locomotive Company (CLC), which built locomotives to Fairbanks-Morse designs; Montreal Locomotive Works (MLW), with Alco designs; and General Motors (GM). Seventy-three diesel locomotives were ordered to replace the 92 steam locomotives used on the two divisions. In practice, the change and its impact was more dramatic because many of the road diesels were booster units that did not require crews.

In 1953 the host of new diesel-electrics began arriving that were to banish steam completely. The program also included passenger and through freight trains running as far east as Medicine Hat, Alberta, and the junction with the main line. The new diesels' rapid takeover of all services was all but complete by the end of September. Only Trains 45 and 46, which were destined for elimination, were assigned steam power on a regular basis. The savings were immense, although many jobs were cut and many people lamented the passing of steam.

The conversion itself was a massive project requiring new facilities including major diesel shops at Nelson. Dieselization also eliminated the need for most roundhouses, water towers and other steam locomotive servicing equipment. As diesels were introduced, crews had to be trained in both operating and servicing the new locomotives. By late summer in 1954, the program was completed and steam had disappeared from all regular Kettle Valley Division assignments.

The diesels permitted many changes in operations and reduced the importance of Penticton as a locomotive servicing centre and base for the train and engine crews. The elimination of helper locomotives meant that crews that had previously worked from Penticton east to Chute Lake or west to Kirton were no longer needed. Similarly, helpers were no longer needed over the Coquihalla. Dieselization was also the beginning of the end for Brookmere as an important terminal on the railway. All normal maintenance of the diesels was concentrated at Nelson and heavy repairs were carried out in Calgary. Only minor work, routine servicing for switchers, wayfreight and work engines, fuel, water and sand were provided at other locations. Locomotives for freight and passenger assignments were based at Nelson and ran through to the coast or east to Medicine Hat.

In purchasing diesels from three different locomotive builders, the CPR gave itself an opportunity to test the new equipment but it also created a maintenance and parts headache. At first, the differing equipment would not function in multiple unit combinations although this problem was eventually rectified. As other dieselization programs were implemented, the CPR began to rationalize the use of the different types of equipment. Most General Motors and Montreal Locomotive Works diesels were assigned elsewhere by the spring of 1957 leaving the Kettle Valley and Kootenay divisions largely the domain of Canadian Locomotive Company units. Yard engines were usually from Montreal Locomotive Works and these were also used on branch lines and work trains.

Diesels were ordered from all three major Canadian builders. These units, the 4469, 4084 and 4084, are Montreal Locomotive Works FA-2s spliced by an FB-2 at Penticton on July 25, 1954. The MLW units were assigned elsewhere later in the 1950s. —JIM HOPE

Yard diesels were used on work trains such as this one with a ditcher near Brodie in September 1953. —ALBERT MARTINO

By 1955 diesel operations were firmly established on the Kettle Valley and Kootenay divisions. The Penticton yards still had the large coaling dock, water tower and sandhouse for steam locomotives. A modern silver-coloured sanding facility for diesels contrasts with the steam-era sandhouse beside the yard diesel, an MLW S-4, No. 7109, on September 4, 1955. —JIM HOPE

"I worked at Brookmere and almost had a steady engineer's job out of Penticton when we got dieselized. But that put me right back to junior fireman after that. I was just down the list, when we got cut into a quarter of the men we had before. A lot of the boys quit, and a lot of them went to the main line."
—*Dick Broccolo*, ENGINEER

"They used to say that the Kettle Valley had about 500 families, all told, from Midway to Hope, that depended on the railway for a living."
—*Bill Quail*, BRAKEMAN

Roadswitchers such as the 8609 became common sights on Kettle Valley freight assignments. These Canadian Locomotive Company Fairbanks-Morse units worked across southern British Columbia until the mid-1970s when they were scrapped. The 8609 was built in December 1956 and replaced diesels from other builders on the Kettle Valley Division. It was photographed near Osoyoos in September 1966. —ROBERT A. LOAT

Two C-Liners work upgrade on a rare beautiful sunny winter's day in Coquihalla Pass. —ALLEN MANUEL, PENTICTON MUSEUM

Dayliners—Rail Diesel Cars—took over the Kettle Valley's passenger services in March 1958. A single car operated twice a week between Penticton and Nelson while one or two cars ran on a daily schedule between Penticton and Vancouver.

At Penticton on September 27, 1958, Train No. 45, with two Dayliners, is nearly ready for its afternoon departure for Princeton, Brookmere, Hope and Vancouver while the other RDC will wait over until the next day to return to Nelson. —JIM HOPE

Dayliner 9023 at Penticton on September 4, 1961. —JIM HOPE

"When they were taking the Dayliners off our parents put us on the train at Penticton and we rode it to Summerland where they picked us up. That was my first train trip." —*Sid Cannings*

One of the washouts that closed the Coquihalla forever. The tracks look more like a suspension bridge than a section of railway. —ALBERT MARTINO COLLECTION

Passenger service also changed with the introduction of diesel power. Initially, Fairbanks-Morse diesels took over pulling the standard passenger rolling stock on an improved schedule. While these changes produced improved service and substantial savings, they were not enough to reverse the change in travel patterns accelerating in the 1950s as more and more people were travelling by highway or by air. Even though travel time was reduced by two hours and 48 minutes between Nelson and Vancouver, the trip still took 21 hours and 40 minutes for the 513 miles (825 km) at an average speed of just over 24 miles (about 37 km) an hour. People had to enjoy leisurely travel or not own a car to go by train.

With each year fewer people used the trains and the provincial highway system was being greatly expanded and improved. Trains 45 and 46 between Vancouver and Penticton were discontinued in 1954 and in October 1957, in anticipation of introducing Rail Diesel Cars (RDCs), passenger service was cut back to provide just coach seating and the Brookmere—Spences Bridge mixed train was discontinued. The through passenger trains lost their "express" designations, sleeping cars and buffet-parlour cars. The *Kettle Valley Express* and the *Kootenay Express* became part of history as did such niceties as the elegance of dining in the buffet-parlour cars. The abbreviated trains were given resurrected Nos. 45 and 46, and at this time, the CPR shifted its less-than-carload freight, mail and express business to trucks, leaving the passenger trains with no supplemental revenue.

In March 1958, the coach trains were replaced by stainless steel RDCs, self-propelled, air-conditioned and efficient. A daily train was retained between Vancouver and Penticton and between Medicine Hat and Nelson, but over the many lonely miles between Nelson and Penticton, there were just two trains a week. The service was clearly designed for local travel; the few passengers wishing to journey across the southern Interior had to make an overnight stop in both Penticton and Nelson when travelling east and in Nelson when travelling west.

Even in the early 1950s, it was clear that there were sections of the Kettle Valley Division that had minimal traffic and they coincided with the most difficult and expensive areas to maintain: Coquihalla Pass and Penticton to Midway. The first major abandonment of trackage came after the closing, due to slides, of the Coquihalla Subdivision in November 1959. With the alternative route through Merritt and Spences Bridge available, the CPR received permission to abandon the trouble-plagued Coquihalla in July 1961. After being open for just 43 years followed by nearly two years of closure, the spectacular mountain crossing was gone. Besides the winter snows and high costs of keeping the line open, the reasons were clear in the traffic statistics and in the changes in economics and operating patterns that had come to the main line and the Kettle Valley Division.

Just as diesels eliminated the need for helpers and doubling trains on the Kettle Valley, they also simplified mainline operations through the Fraser and Thompson canyons between Ruby Creek and Spences Bridge. Grades there had reduced the haulage capacity of steam locomotives by half. Fred Joplin, Kettle Valley roadmaster and division engineer, later CPR vice-president of operations and maintenance, explained some of the changes that came in the 1950s:

"Diesels had come in and could handle bigger trains and could run to Spences Bridge without much additional cost. With diesels we could get our tonnage out of Vancouver to Spences Bridge. Previously, freight trains were broken up at Ruby Creek. You would run out of Vancouver with a train that contained both mainline and KV tonnage and drop it off at Ruby. We'd run caboose hops from North Bend to Ruby Creek and then back up to North Bend [to handle the tonnage brought into Ruby Creek by one engine].

"When we started to run diesels we dropped that kind of operation. We ran full trains out of Vancouver and didn't need to set off tonnage at Ruby Creek. We could take the KV tonnage through to Spences Bridge at really little additional cost. That, and maintaining the Coquihalla was difficult and unreliable."

John Favrin was roadmaster at Brookmere in 1959. "The fall rains would get us. You'd get a snowfall of maybe six inches or a foot, then it would turn mild and start raining. Then everything would let go. That's what happened in '59. There was a bridge where the washout occurred and a fill. A culvert plugged up with sand . . . in four or five hours it was completely washed out." —JOHN FAVRIN COLLECTION

The decision to close the Coquihalla was reached after the CPR had considered a broad view of the future of the Kettle Valley and rail operations across southern British Columbia. In August 1961 another major change came with the diversion of nearly all through freight to the main line. The largest generator of traffic was the Cominco smelter and fertilizer plant at Trail and vicinity. This heavy tonnage was routed east to Cranbrook and then north over the Windermere Subdivision to the main line at Golden. From there, the products moved west; through-traffic over the Kettle Valley all but disappeared. It was cheaper to consolidate traffic and move it a longer distance over the essentially flat trackage to Golden than deal with the twisting, slow route and heavy grades of the Kettle Valley and Kootenay divisions. The declining importance of the Kettle Valley was underlined when it lost its status as a separate CPR division on July 1, 1962. Trackage east of Penticton became part of the Kootenay Division, the line through to Spences Bridge came under the Canyon Division, but the Penticton yard and the Osoyoos Subdivision were assigned to the Revelstoke Division.

The closing of the Coquihalla had an immediate impact on the already minimal passenger service. Although the same frequency of trains was maintained, the service became even less attractive to travellers. The trains no longer ran directly through to Vancouver but instead connections were provided at Spences Bridge with Trains 7 and 8. The October 1961 timetable shows that eastbound passengers had to board the Kettle Valley train in Spences Bridge at

The last passenger train at Rock Creek on January 17, 1964. —ERIC SISMEY, PENTICTON MUSEUM, 37-3875

"You had the buses and the freight lines coming in and the airlines were taking the passengers and it just reduced the earnings of the stations to beat the band. Then they cut out the passenger trains. The jobs disappeared." —*Reid Johnston*, WEST SUMMERLAND STATION AGENT, 1926-1952

2:50 a.m. while those travelling west arrived at 12:15 a.m. and departed 15 minutes later for Vancouver. Citing losses of $510,000 for 1962, the CPR was granted permission to discontinue the RDCs and in January 1964 the passenger service on the Kettle Valley route and on through Nelson and the Crowsnest was ended.

Two years later, on August 1, 1966, the once busy crew terminal of Brookmere was eliminated and train crews ran through to either Spences Bridge or Penticton. The community that had grown around the needs of the steam locomotives and their hard-working crews all but faded away.

THE FINAL YEARS

"With the end of the fruit traffic over the barge we were left with lumber, chips and gasoline and fuel oil and propane. It got to the point where the railway put a slow order of 10 miles per hour for trains handling fuel oil or empty tank cars; that made the run from Spences Bridge terribly long." —*L. S. Morrison*, OPERATOR AT PENTICTON

Traffic continued to decline in the 1970s and the decade saw the abandonment of large sections of the Kettle Valley's trackage. The railway barge service from Kelowna to Penticton and other lake points was discontinued at the end of May 1972. Increasingly, commercial freight, and in particular the highly valuable, perishable fruit traffic, was all moved by truck. Freight traffic had dwindled to such low levels to the east of Penticton that the next year service was suspended between Penticton and Beaverdell over most of the Carmi Subdivision including the famous route through Myra Canyon. The last use of the Carmi Subdivision was for filming in June 1973 of the Canadian Broadcast Corporation's series *The National Dream*, based on the books by Pierre Berton. Occasional trains continued to run as far west as Beaverdell. Formal approval to abandon all the trackage between Midway and Penticton was given at the end of 1978 and the tracks were removed over the next two years despite hopes to retain some sections for excursions or other uses. Losses of $341,048 against a revenue of only $48,442 were determined by the Railway Transport Committee for 1976. As business diminished and passenger services ended, the need for many small stations passed and most were closed. Some stations, including those at Oliver, Osoyoos, Midway and Penticton, were preserved for other community functions amid a growing public awareness of the possible recreational and cultural uses of the railway.

Eventually, the only substantial traffic remaining between Spences Bridge and Penticton was lumber and wood chips. Service south of Okanagan Falls was discontinued after the Provincial Museum train toured in the summer of 1977 and the trackage was formally abandoned in 1978. The trackage along Skaha Lake was retained so that the Weyerhaeuser mill at Okanagan Falls could continue to ship lumber by rail. Operating patterns varied, but the 1980s saw service slowly decline to two trains a week and finally to even less frequent operations. By the end of the decade, trains were often as short as two engines with three or four cars and a caboose winding their lonely way east over the Jura Loops to Penticton.

The CPR stopped running trains between Midway and Penticton in 1973 but service continued until 1977 to Beaverdell, where the 8603 was photographed in spring 1974. —ROBERT D. TURNER

The final blow to the Penticton Subdivision, as the last major remnant of the KVR was then known, came in 1988 with the announcement by CP Rail that it was establishing a large lumber loading terminal at Campbell Creek a few miles east of Kamloops. Any mills in the south Okanagan, Princeton and Merritt areas could truck lumber to the terminal for reloading onto railcars. This would permit the elimination of train service over the entire route from Spences Bridge.

The late winter and spring days of 1989 marked the last runs. On March 1, the last freight train left Penticton for Merritt and over the next few months only work trains operated east of Princeton. By the end of April, service to Princeton had ceased and on Tuesday, May 9, the last work train, picking up any remaining equipment, left Penticton and ran through to Merritt. That Friday, May 12, the final clean-up train left Merritt for the main line at Spences Bridge and the curtain fell over the Kettle Valley. Another year passed before Canadian Pacific was given authority to abandon the trackage. Dismantling, with the important exception of 16 km (10 miles) between Trout Creek Canyon and Faulder, saved at public insistence, followed. From the gradual abandonment of the Kettle Valley came growing public awareness of its potential as heritage sites, recreational corridors and trails, and as a steam railway. These developments, which provide a glimpse of the future of the Kettle Valley, are highlighted on the following pages.

A snowplow extra running to Penticton in the final years of service on the Kettle Valley. —LANCE CAMP

The British Columbia Provincial Museum's Museum Train brought steam back to the Kettle Valley for a brief appearance in July 1977 when it toured as far south as Osoyoos. It was the last train to operate south of Okanagan Falls. The next year it also visited Midway. At Penticton, locomotive 3716 steams beside two other veterans. —LANCE CAMP

Four miles east of Princeton, a long freight winds its way eastbound from Spences Bridge and Merritt. Two General Motors GP9R diesels were the locomotives on July 30, 1968. Over a decade later, on August 11, 1979, below right, representatives of a newer generation of diesels wind along the Nicola River six miles east of Spences Bridge with cars for Merritt, Princeton and Penticton.
—ROBERT A. LOAT

In the waning years of service on the Carmi Subdivision, Train No. 71, a westbound Midway-to-Penticton scheduled freight, stops at Chute Lake on July 10, 1971, before descending the long grade into Penticton. —ROBERT A. LOAT

Over the years, interest in the tunnels grew and in July 1987, after considerable work including the replacement of one bridge and the installation of decking and railings to the second, the site was dedicated as the Coquihalla Canyon Recreation Area by the province. Katie Turner looks down into the Coquihalla Canyon in July 1995. —ROBERT D. TURNER

The Quintette Tunnels were a highlight of the Kettle Valley from the earliest days of the railway. The great rock bluffs dwarfed the trains as in this scene, from about 1951. The tunnels and the canyon marked the transition from the mountains to the east and the Fraser Valley to the west. —NICHOLAS MORANT

EPILOGUE

Many Mountains to Cross— The Kettle Valley Railway Heritage

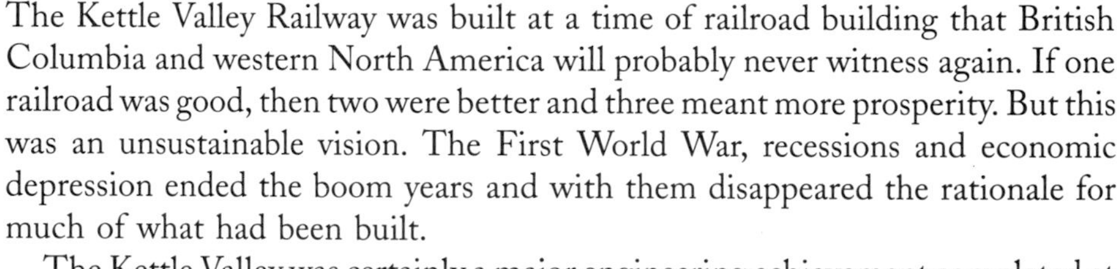

The Kettle Valley Railway was built at a time of railroad building that British Columbia and western North America will probably never witness again. If one railroad was good, then two were better and three meant more prosperity. But this was an unsustainable vision. The First World War, recessions and economic depression ended the boom years and with them disappeared the rationale for much of what had been built.

The Kettle Valley was certainly a major engineering achievement completed at a time when steam-era railway building was at its zenith just before the First World War. Over 30 years of railroading experience in the Coast Range, Rockies and Selkirks, as well as knowledge gained on the Great Northern and Northern Pacific in the Cascades a short distance to the south, gave the engineers led by Andrew McCulloch, a firm base of construction and operating experience to draw upon. But the railway, for all its creative and imaginative engineering and high cost construction, was not one destined for ease of operation or low operating costs. The Kettle Valley never had the traffic to justify the extensive improvements necessary to protect the line through the Coquihalla or to reduce its grades by line revisions or tunnelling. Moreover, the Kettle Valley was connected to just too many other sections of heavy mountain grade to the east all the way through the Crowsnest Pass. Even extensive work in the Coquihalla Pass would not have solved its problems. In the end, the Kettle Valley was burdened by too many obstacles to survive the competition coming with massive expansion of the highway system after the Second World War.

Ultimately British Columbia by-passed the Kettle Valley Railway. A pre-First World War railway, albeit modernized with diesel power, could not provide the level of service expected by travellers or businesses in the 1980s. The Coquihalla Highway, completed in 1986, and it extension to the Okanagan demonstrated the point. In about two hours, one could travel by car from Hope to Kelowna. In 1955 it took the *Kettle Valley Express* seven hours and ten minutes to reach Penticton from Hope on an overnight schedule. The flexibility provided by automobiles was, for most people, so much more appealing than the fixed departures of trains.

The relatively short life of the Kettle Valley line reflects the accelerating technological change during the 20th century. Motor vehicles were not an important means of travel in Canada when the decision was reached to build the

Kettle Valley station mile boards preserved as part of historical exhibits in museums at Hope, Summerland and Penticton.
—ROBERT D. TURNER; RANDY MANUEL

Max Jacquiard
©

Canadian
Pacific

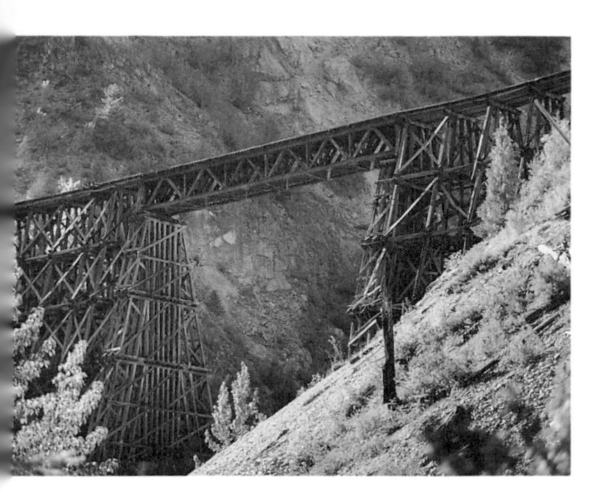

Long after the last trains ran through the Coquihalla, many reminders of the railway survived. This is the bridge over Fallslake Creek, west of the site of Coquihalla Station. August 1995.
—ROBERT D. TURNER

Three CP Rail GP38 diesels ease down grade over Trout Creek Bridge towards Penticton with empty woodchip and lumber cars on a beautiful April 22, 1980.
—ROBERT A. LOAT

In January 1989, with just a few months left before the closing of the railway, an eastbound freight climbs towards Osprey Lake from Princeton through a bitter cold and windswept landscape.
—ROBERT D. TURNER

The *Kootenay Express* crosses Trout Creek on a beautiful Okanagan morning in the early 1950s. Max Jacquiard's beautiful painting was completed especially for this book. —MAX JACQUIARD

railway but within a decade of its completion they were already eroding the traffic base for railroads. The first aircraft flights in British Columbia occurred within a year or two of the beginning of construction. Few would have guessed the role of aviation by the end of the Second World War or that Canadian Pacific, even though at first reluctantly, would be establishing itself in the airline business. The short useful life of branch lines does not mean that they were neither necessary nor useful. They were also victims of the change they had helped to nourish.

The Kettle Valley was the setting for 50 years of magnificent struggle—the struggle of railroaders moving trains through the mountains in some of the worst winter weather imaginable and of repairing tracks and bridges time after time. It is difficult to imagine how something as complex and important as the Kettle Valley Railway can cease to exist so quickly and completely. Men who started their careers when the Kettle Valley was new were there to see the last passenger train. Some saw the end of the railway a generation later.

The name Kettle Valley Railway itself helped to distinguish the KVR from other scenic and interesting parts of the CPR system. Its independence, often more imagined than real, also set it apart from the huge transcontinental. The spectacular locations, particularly the Othello Tunnels, Coquihalla Pass, Trout Creek and Myra Canyon, brought further fame and laid the basis for its future as a heritage resource. For all that, the Kettle Valley would not have worked at all without the determination and hard work of a generation of railroaders and their families who accepted the Coquihalla as a challenge, who walked the tops of the boxcars in driving snowstorms to knock down the brake retainers, who hand-fired the steam locomotives on countless McCulloch Turns or who patrolled and maintained the tracks through blistering heat or penetrating, numbing cold.

This book ends with a beginning, a point where parts of a railway have been reopened to a new generation for reasons far different from those that prompted its original construction in the early 1900s. Freight and mail are gone from the railway and there is no longer a worry about competition from the northern extensions of a large American transcontinental. Yet in some ways the purpose of the KVR remains similar. From its beginning the original Kettle Valley Railway depended heavily on passengers and the underlying purpose of the railway was as an economic stimulus to the regions through which it passed. In these ways the heritage sites, the trail through Myra Canyon and the Kettle Valley Steam Railway are akin to their predecessor and their future will depend on public enjoyment and recreation. Just as the original Kettle Valley Railway did, the KVR in the future will make important contributions to the economy and lifestyle of the Okanagan and Southern British Columbia.

The Myra Canyon Trail

The 16 trestles and two bridges through Myra Canyon high above Kelowna highlighted one of the most spectacular sections of the Kettle Valley Railway. They became a focus for outstanding preservation efforts by the Myra Canyon Restoration Society, after earlier attempts to save the tracks failed. The acquisition of the right-of-way by the province, an enormous volunteer effort and major donations of materials and labour resulted in the stabilization of the bridges, the installation of new decking and guard rails and the opening of the trail in September 1995. Often service clubs or companies sponsored a bridge for reconstruction. It is one of the outstanding walking and cycling trails in North America. Many sections of the right-of-way are accessible including much of the grade from Penticton with its tunnels and other reminders of the railway's story. —ROBERT D. TURNER

The Kettle Valley Steam Railway

After attempts at preserving parts of the Kettle Valley failed, the Kettle Valley Railway Heritage Society was formed in 1989 at the instigation of Arthur Halsted of Okanagan Falls. Many volunteers, businesses, organizations and provincial and federal government agencies became committed to the project. An agreement between the society, the Ministry of Small Business, Tourism and Culture, and the B.C. Forest Museum at Duncan provided the stimulus for the opening of the railway in 1995.

The loan of former Mayo Lumber No. 3, a 1924 Shay logging locomotive, from the B.C. Forest Museum was a major step in returning steam to the Kettle Valley. Three former CPR passenger cars from BC Rail's Royal Hudson train provided the first rolling stock. More equipment will be needed and one day, perhaps, a former CPR locomotive will once again run on the Kettle Valley.

Heritage preservation is more than completing a restoration. It requires maintaining public interest, commitment and enjoyment. It is a tribute to the past, based on a conviction that some things are truly worth maintaining and continuing. A leap of imagination and creativity is often needed to see what something can become when often all that one sees is the neglected remains of something that was. This vision and optimism is responsible for saving our most worthwhile landmarks, such as the *Sicamous* and parts of the Kettle Valley Railway.

The Kettle Valley Railway deserves to be preserved as a monument to all those who worked on it or depended on its services but perhaps even more importantly, riding the trains through the orchard lands of the southern Okanagan, hiking through Myra Canyon or exploring the Othello tunnels is a wonderful and pleasurable thing to do. Just as early travellers of the Kettle Valley found, picnics, family outings or group excursions by train are indeed special, as is the aura of a working steam locomotive and the echo of its whistle through the mountains. The Kettle Valley is too important to forget and just too good to let slip away.

Shay No. 3 was restored at the B.C. Forest Museum at Duncan on Vancouver Island and was nearly complete by early May 1995. The restoration crew, at right, included: Pat Clarkson, Beatty Davis, John G. Smith, Bob Symington, Doug Meer, Pat Hosford (above), Ron Cooke, George Williamson, Wayne Nolan and Glen Wheeler. Mayo Lumber No. 3 spent about 20 years working in the Cowichan Valley before being preserved by the Mayo family at Paldi. In the mid-1960s it was moved to the Forest Museum. —ROBERT D. TURNER

Shay No. 3 steamed to West Summerland from the Trout Creek Bridge to reopen the railway to passenger service on September 17, 1995. A large, welcoming crowd was on hand including dignitaries and many who remembered the Kettle Valley of old and many who were not old enough to remember. —ROBERT D. TURNER

Overheard in the crowd:

"To see that steam and to hear that whistle—what a thrill. What a shame they pulled up all that track, nobody thinks ahead in this country."

"We could hear the whistle in Naramata. . . ."

"Forty years ago, you could hear them all through the night working up to Chute Lake. The whistles would just resonate through the hills. . . ."

"I remember in the '30s, seeing the men who were out of work riding the freight trains. Then the war came and they were all gone. . . ."

"Can I pleassse go on the train???" —YOUNGSTER ABOUT FOUR YEARS OLD

"Leaving Penticton, the line skirts along the edge of the West Summerland Valley, one of the most prolific fruit-growing districts of Canada. The entrance to this valley is guarded by 'The Giant's Head,' a rock projection of gigantic proportions. Leaving the valley, Trout Creek is reached through a picturesque canyon, a deep gorge in solid rock. . . ." —*The Lake Districts of Southern British Columbia*, 1919, ROBERT W. PARKINSON COLLECTION

Index

SUMMARY INDEX TO PEOPLE, PLACES AND SELECTED TOPICS

Further Reading

Burrows, Roger G. 1984. *Railway Mileposts: British Columbia. Vol. II: The Southern Routes from the Crowsnest to the Coquihalla.* Railway Milepost Books, North Vancouver, B.C.

Eagle, Don. 1989. *The Canadian Pacific Railway and the Development of Western Canada.* McGill-Queen's University Press, Kingston, Ont.

Hill, Beth. 1989. *Exploring the Kettle Valley Railway.* Polestar Press, Winlaw, B.C.

Kennedy, W. G. 1986. *Canadian Pacific in Southern British Columbia, The Boundary Subdivision.* BRMNA, Calgary, Alberta.

Langford, Don and Sandra. 1994. *Cycling the Kettle Valley Railway.* Rocky Mountain Books, Calgary, Alberta.

Lavallée, Omer. 1985. *Canadian Pacific Steam Locomotives.* Railfare Enterprises, Toronto, Ont.

Mattheson, George. 1994. *The Vaders' Caboose.* Kettle Valley Publishers, Lumby, B.C. (with Frank and Zelma Vader)

Riegger, Hal. 1981. *The Kettle Valley and Its Railways.* Pacific Fast Mail, Edmonds, WA.

Sanford, Barrie. 1977. *McCulloch's Wonder, The Story of the Kettle Valley Railway.* Whitecap Books, West Vancouver, B.C.

———. 1990. *Steel Rails and Iron Men, A Pictorial History of the Kettle Valley Railway.* Whitecap Books, Vancouver, B.C.

Turner, Robert D. 1981. *Railroaders, Recollections from the Steam Era.* Sound Heritage Series No. 31, Provincial Archives of British Columbia, Victoria, B.C.

———. 1984. *Sternwheelers & Steam Tugs. An Illustrated History of the Canadian Pacific Railway's British Columbia Lake & River Service.* Sono Nis Press, Victoria, B.C.

———. 1987. *West of the Great Divide. An Illustrated History of the Canadian Pacific Railway in British Columbia 1880-1986.* Sono Nis Press, Victoria, B.C.

———. 1995. *The Sicamous and the Naramata. Steamboat Days in the Okanagan.* Sono Nis Press (in cooperation with the SS Sicamous Society and the Royal B.C. Museum), Victoria, B.C.

Turner, Robert D. and David Wilkie. 1995. *The Skyline Limited, The Kaslo & Slocan Railway.* Sono Nis Press, Victoria, B.C.

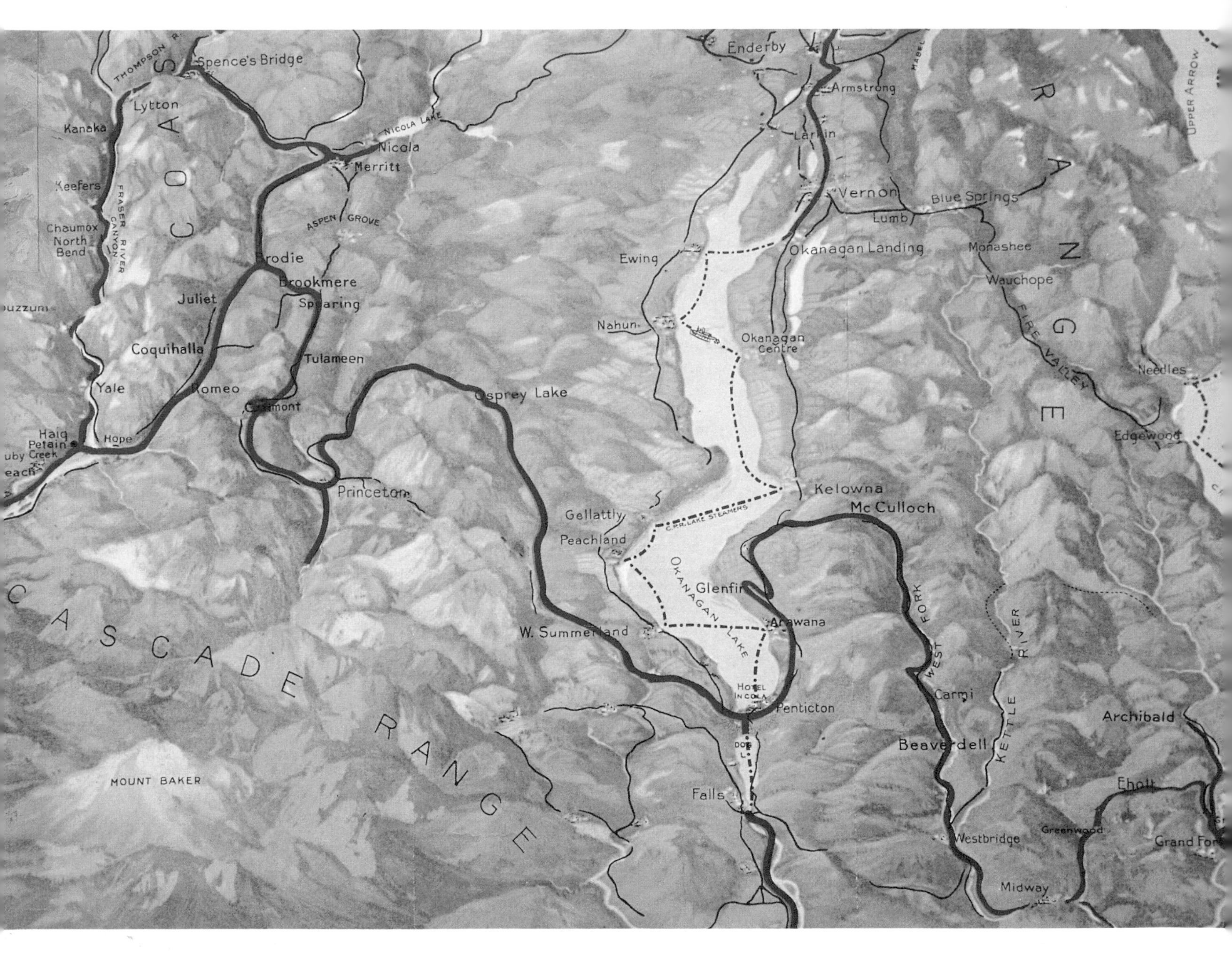

 From: "Panoramic Map of the Canadian Pacific Rockies," produced by the CPR in 1925. —BENNING COLLECTION, ROYAL B.C. MUSEUM, 990.1.40